THE
FINANCIAL SECTOR
OF THE AMERICAN
ECONOMY

edited by

STUART BRUCHEY
UNIVERSITY OF MAINE

A GARLAND SERIES

A STRATEGIC ANALYSIS OF THE UNITED STATES BANKING INDUSTRY

AJAY MEHRA

GARLAND PUBLISHING, INC.
NEW YORK & LONDON / 1995

Library of Congress Cataloging-in-Publication Data

Mehra, Ajay.
  A strategic analysis of the United States banking industry /
Ajay Mehra.
      p.   cm. — (The Financial sector of the American
economy)
  Includes bibliographical references and index.
  ISBN 0-8153-2007-8 (alk. paper)
  1. Banks and banking—United States.   2. Competition—
United States.   I. Title.   II. Series.
HG2491.M44   1995
332.1'0973—dc20   95-16134
                                                       CIP

Printed on acid-free, 250-year-life paper
Manufactured in the United States of America

To my parents who always encouraged me to chase my dreams.

Contents

INTRODUCTION

The basic function of a banking firm is financial intermediation and its core product is making loans and accepting deposits. Due to the underlying commodity nature of this product the opportunities for product differentiation and value creation available to firms in this industry are rather limited. This problem is further compounded by the absence of patents and the transparency of the production process, which restricts the availability of first mover advantages. Thus, in absence of regulatory protection or market imperfections, it is difficult to sustain competitive advantage in this industry.

The banking industry has undergone tremendous changes in recent years brought upon by the forces of deregulation, technological developments, and globalization. These changes have provided much greater opportunities for competitive differentiation and have led to a significant increase in the degree of competition in this previously regulated and largely uniform industry. In essence the economics of the industry has changed from being supply driven to being demand led.

Along with the increase in the intensity of competition there has been a concomitant shift in the nature or the basis of competition. While previously competition focused on preemptive entry into key geographical and product markets to establish advantage, now it focuses more on developing key organizational resources and capabilities such as innovation, efficient production process, strong credit culture etc., since these are the only durable sources of advantage.

What happens to the underlying competitive structure in an industry when it goes through competence destroying changes? Do certain core positions, deep structures, or old formulae persist despite revolutionary changes? Are managerial actions redundant in the face of sudden changes or should executives actively manage the process of industry transformation?

This study addresses some of these questions in the context of the U.S. banking industry. Banking faced revolutionary changes beginning in 1980 and may therefore provide a unique retrospective into a period of disequilibrium. The research traces the patterns of profiles associated with various business strategies in the U.S. banking industry over a fifteen year period. It fundamentally attempts to uncover the determinants of competitive advantage in this industry by examining the rationale for the consistently superior performance of some firms over time. Using a combination of data based and a field based clinical research design with explicit involvement of leading industry analysts, it documents the shifting bases of competition in the U.S. banking industry.

A lot has been written about the trials, tribulations, and the recent comeback of the U.S. banking industry. However, most of that work overlooks the fundamental shifts taking place in the competitive stratagem of this industry and paradigm shifts that are required to succeed in the emerging global marketplace. I use the concepts and methodologies developed in the field of strategic management to examine the performance and strategy profiles of "winners" and "losers" in this industry.

On a broader level, this strategic analysis focuses on one fundamental question: Why are some firms consistently more profitable than others? Developing an understanding into the determinants of superior performance has fascinated strategy scholars since the beginnings of the field. Indeed, it is the fact of these persistent inter-firm performance differences that was the origin of the strategy concept (Rumelt, Schendel & Teece, 1991). Other important questions such as why firms differ, how they behave, how they choose strategies, and how they are managed, are subsumed by this one overarching question (Porter, 1991).

Early researchers working in the tradition of the Mason/Bain structure-conduct-performance (SCP) paradigm, attributed differential firm performance to the structural nature of the industry. Beginning in the seventies, strategy researchers started looking for answers within the industry and modified the SCP to advance the concept of strategic groups and mobility barriers to account for intraindustry heterogeneity and performance variation. This framework argues that stable persistent firm profits derive from the economic structure within industries and that the primary source of stable differences in firm profitability within industries is strategic group membership and its associated collective behavior (Caves & Porter, 1977, Porter 1979). However, despite numerous empirical efforts to test the performance implications associated with group membership, no conclusive evidence exists for the hypothesized group-performance linkage.

Recently, strategic management has developed the theory of the resource based view (RBV) of the firm. According to the resource based theorists (Penrose, 1959; Wernerfelt, 1984; Peteraf, 1993), bundles of resources, rather than the product market combinations chosen for their deployment, lie at the heart of a firm's competitive advantage. This approach calls for viewing the firm not through its activities in the product market but as a unique bundle of tangible and intangible resources. RBV shifts attention away from product-market barriers to competition, and towards factor-market impediments to resource flows. To the extent that new competition is resource based, RBV suggests a complementary way of identifying strategic groups and in turn of investigating the causality of persistent interfirm performance differences within the same industry.

In the first phase, using data from the Bank Compustat database and a sophisticated clustering algorithm, eleven variables measuring business scope and resource deployment strategies are employed to stratify rival firms into strategic groups. The fifteen year study horizon is broken down into six subperiods of relative stability within the industry. Changes in strategic group structure and membership in each of these subperiods are then used to investigate the dynamics of intraindustry competition and firm risk-return relationships. Clear evidence of economic performance and risk differences was found across different strategic groups which essentially represent different competitive strategies in the industry. However, when individual strategic postures were adjusted for the risk that each strategy entailed, performance differences evaporated. In the second phase, scores obtained through semi-structured interviews from an expert panel of leading bank analysts on ten key resources are used to identify an alternative set of resource based strategic groups.

The study found that firm resources and capabilities which included management quality and depth, asset quality, franchise, placing power, risk management, innovation, adequacy of the capital base, informational asymmetries, etc. accounted for about 51% of the performance variation within the industry, while market positions explained about 13% of differential performance. This provides evidence for the increasing importance of the firm resources and capabilities in determining competitive success in the banking industry. The findings also validate the predictions of the RBV theory and shed some new light on the strategic group-performance linkage.

A longitudinal analysis revealed that firms frequently changed their strategic positions after the partial deregulation of the industry in 1980. However, not all strategic shifts were successful. In some instances, there was a lagging response to the opportunities afforded by deregulation. This may have resulted due to inertia and slow decision making processes of some of the larger institutions. There was a clear evidence of a "herd-mentality" in the industry. As one firm changed its strategic posture, other firms in the group quickly followed suit, without adequately reflecting on either the suitability of new strategy or their capability to execute it.

The primary import of this research for bankers is the need to shift their strategic focus from privileged product market positions as the basis of competitive advantage to creating, nurturing, and sustaining key resources. Ten such resources are identified and defined in the book. This shift in focus also calls for supplementing their existing mental models of competition to include competitors in the factor markets, who are often not their rivals in the product markets. A key finding is that risk management is a core skill in the banking industry. And simply investing in state-of-art technological systems and financial engineering departments/products does not payoff unless management has the depth and vision to properly deploy these resources. A strong capital base is also necessary for creation of a sustainable competitive advantage. Finally, a longitudinal examination of performance and strategy profiles shows that the strategic logic of this industry favors either low cost producers or highly focused players.

Acknowledgments

This study has benefitted from the support and insights of many people. My greatest intellectual and personal debt is to Professor Steve Floyd. Professor Floyd has been my friend, philosopher, and guide throughout my scholarly journey. He constantly challenged my thinking and encouraged me to break new ground. Professor W.G. Shepherd was instrumental in stimulating my interest in I.O. economics, and setting high standards of excellence for my scholarly endeavors. I would like to thank Dean Tom O'Brien and Professor Tom Scheenewis of the University of Massachusetts at Amherst, where this study was conducted, for opening doors and providing access to a large number of investment banks.

To the industry experts who participated in this study and gave very generously of their valuable time, especially Thomas Hanley of First Boston Corporation (formerly of Salomon Brothers) who deepened my understanding of this industry, I shall remain eternally grateful. Finally, I would like to thank my graduate assistant: Eric Johnson - who patiently worked through various iterations of the manuscript and expertly formatted and edited the final version.

Illustrations

TABLES

FIGURES

A Strategic
Analysis of the
United States
Banking Industry

Chapter I
Overview

Few concepts have sparked as much interest and debate among strategy researchers as the concept of strategic groups. In fact it has become one of the dominant areas of empirical research in strategic management (Barney & Hoskissen, 1990). Yet, after twenty years since Hunt (1972) originally coined the term strategic groups to describe competition in the white goods industry and some thirty odd studies later, three fundamental questions regarding the existence, stability and performance implications of strategic groups remain unresolved.

The question of existence is largely ontological, and intimately tied to the stability and performance issues. To substantiate claims that strategic groups are an integral part of industry structure requires, longitudinal designs demonstrating stable groups under a variety of environmental circumstances. However, out of all the empirical studies to date only Oster (1982), Cool (1985), Fiegenbaum (1987), and Mascarenhas (1989) tested for the stability of derived groupings. Even among these four studies, the methodologies employed by Oster (1982) and Mascarenhas (1989) are quite different from the other two. Therefore, a key impediment in addressing these questions arises due to the nonuniformity of methodologies employed in the studies of strategic groups.

The empirical findings on the performance implications of strategic groups are conflicting and extremely confusing (Caves & Pugel 1980, Porter 1979, Cool & Schendel 1987, Fiegenbaum & Thomas 1990). This could be because most studies were data driven (Mcgee & Thomas, 1986), and have employed under-specified models to test across group performance differences. Alternatively, within group performance variance, due to firm level capability differences, may have dwarfed across group variation (Cool & Schendel, 1988). In addition, most studies failed to carefully operationalize the multifaceted nature of the performance construct (Fiegenbaum & Thomas 1990).

The linkage of strategic groups and performance is a focal point in the strategic groups literature (Caves & Porter, 1977; Porter, 1979; Cool & Schendel 1987). The inconclusive empirical evidence on this issue means that either no such linkage exists or that the relationship has not been captured due to under/poor specification of the model.

Taking the specification issue as paramount, this study examines alternative sets of group defining variables. In the first model, variables are derived that measure scope and resource deployment strategies. Drawing on the methodology in Cool (1985) and Fiegenbaum and Thomas (1990), these variables are used in a longitudinal analysis of strategic groups over the period 1974-1988. Beyond replicating the approach taken in these previous studies, it takes advantage of special circumstances in the banking industry to examine the effects of discontinuous change (i.e. deregulation & LDC debt crises) on inter-group mobility, and firm level risk-return relationships, as well as performance differences between and within groups.

The second model employs resource-based theory (Wernerfelt, 1984; Barney, 1991). Measures of ten capabilities are obtained from an expert panel of leading investment analysts and are used in a cross-sectional investigation of industry heterogeneity. This analysis explores resource-based clusters as a means for specifying strategic groups and compares capabilities with scope and resource deployment variables in accounting for intraindustry performance differences.

This study, therefore, seeks to conceptually redefine the focus of the strategic groups research by exploring a contrasting theory of groups which facilitates an evaluation of existing approaches to model specification and analysis. In addition, it addresses an unresolved and contentious debate in the literature by extending the longitudinal analysis of strategic groups to the banking industry, thereby seeking confirmation for the results in previous studies (Cool, 1985; Fiegenbaum, 1987) and, for the first time, examining the effects of discontinuous change on group dynamics. Finally, it employs measures of firm capabilities along with positioning strategies to comprehensively test the strategy-performance linkage.

Four research questions provide a structure for grouping seven hypotheses. They are detailed below:

1.   What are the dynamic patterns of strategic group formation and movement over a period of time? What is the impact of

discontinuous environmental change on inter-group mobility and firm level risk-return relationships?

2. What is the nature of the relationship between strategic group membership and firm performance?

3. Does the gap between capabilities and strategy account for the variation in measures of firm performance?

4. Are firm resource bundles better predictors of strategic group membership than observed product market strategies?

1.1 OUTLINE OF THE STUDY

To examine these research questions, this study is organized into seven chapters. Chapter II lays down the theoretical background of the strategic group and the mobility barriers concept. It begins by reviewing the existing literature. This reviews culminates by highlighting the unresolved questions in this line of enquiry. Then drawing on the resource based view of the firm, an alternative view of strategic groups is proposed.

Chapter III states the research questions and hypotheses. An explanation/justification follows each question and hypothesis. Chapter IV describes the research design and methodology adopted in this study. To enhance expositional clarity, the description is broken down into the longitudinal facet and the cross-sectional facet. Chapter V presents the results of this study, outlining the procedures followed for testing individual hypotheses and detailing the findings. The chapter ends by discussing the limitations of empirical results.

Chapter VI discusses the results, comparing them with previous studies, highlighting both similarities and differences in the findings, and expounding on the significance of the findings for the strategic groups research in particular, and strategic management research in general. Finally, Chapter VII summarizes the findings and details the theoretical and methodological contributions of this study to strategy research. The chapter ends by discussing the implications of this study for the banking industry.

Chapter II
Theoretical Framework: Strategic Groups and Mobility Barriers

Competition has been the central pillar of research in strategic management and arguably its most important concern. One of the most important foundations of the competitive model that is put into question by theories of imperfect competition is that, in order to be considered as price takers, the number of agents needs to be sufficiently large. In contrast, a situation of oligopoly, in which a small number of firms face a large number of buyers, implies a strategic interdependence between sellers, such that the best policy for a firm will depend on that followed by each of its competitors. In this context the anonymity of competition disappears, and economic agents become players. It is this oligopolistic competitive context which is the domain of strategic management, an assumption which is rarely explicitly stated.

Industrial organization economics (IO) theory suggests that some key structural characteristics condition the firm's range of choices of competitive strategy in the market (i.e. the firm's conduct). Oligopoly theory seeks to clarify and explain the link between structure and conduct (firm-to-firm rivalry). Unfortunately, most of the research in IO tradition has focused on the structure - performance link with conduct being solved out as a mere intervening variable. The standard Structure - Conduct - Performance model of IO is based on the assumption of homogenous industries, and its explanatory power collapses in a sample of heterogenous industries. Hatten, Schendel & Cooper (1978) have warned that industry level models and indiscriminate pooling of data leads to results that can easily mislead if used at the firm level. Based on their study of brewing industry, they conclude: "Generally, a comparison of industry versus group-level equations reveals a number of instances where the consequences of the business strategies followed by specific groups of brewers differ, and certainly differ from the "averaging" and perhaps misleading industry estimates. Different firms can (and must) use different resource deployments to compete successfully" (Hatten, Schendel & Cooper, 1978 : 604). The strategic group literature within the IO discipline has evolved from the belief that there are more conduct differences between firms than just size. (Cool 1985:18).

2.1 THEORETICAL UNDERPINNINGS

In this section I dwell on the theoretical rationale for the existence of intraindustry heterogeneity and its attendant implications. Specifically, I address three constructs related to the existence of strategic groups: (1) mobility barriers, (2) firm performance differences and (3) competitive rivalry. The focus is on the utility of these constructs for enhancing our understanding of competition within industries.

2.1.1 Early Definition

The term strategic groups was coined by Michael Hunt (1972) in his study of the white goods industry. He found that industry participants differed on three key strategic dimensions: degree of vertical integration, degree of product diversification, and the extent of product differentiation. Based on these dimensions he isolated four groups: (1) full line national manufacturer's brand producers, (2) part line manufacturers' brand producers, (3) private brands producers, and (4) national retailers. Hunt believed this taxonomy "minimized economic asymmetry in each group and revealed barriers to entry to each strategic group" (Hunt, 1972:57). He defined strategic groups as:

> "A group of firms within an industry that are highly symmetric....with respect to cost structure, degree of product diversification ... formal organization, control systems, and management rewards and punishments ...(and) the personal views and preferences for various possible outcomes ...." (Hunt, 1972: 8).

Newman (1973,1978), in his study of chemical process industries identified strategic groups by the relationship between the industry at one hand and the activities carried out by its member firms outside that industry, on the other hand, with firms sharing the same basic business being placed in the same strategic group. He concluded that "differing base industries and patterns of vertical integration sufficed to stratify rival sellers into subgroups" (Newman, 1978 pg.425). He further attempts to define strategic groups by noting :

> "If corporate strategies can differ persistently among direct market rivals, then we can speak of strategic groups - each group consisting of firms highly symmetric in their corporate strategies as a stable element of market structures."

Full scale theoretical development of the concept was done by Porter (1976,1979,1980), who focused on intraindustry heterogeneity in the retail distribution industry and concluded that "An industry can thus be viewed as composed of clusters or groups of firms, where each group consists of firms following similar strategies in terms of the key decision variables. Such a group could consist of a single firm, or could encompass all the firms in the industry. I define such groups as strategic groups" (Porter, 1979: 215).

The presence of strategic groups within an industry was expected to affect industry performance through the process of competitive rivalry between groups and differential barriers to entry between groups. Groups which were protected by higher barriers and were relatively insulated from the process of competitive rivalry within the industry were expected to enjoy superior performance. Firms within a strategic group were presumed to recognize their mutual dependence much more closely and react similarly to disturbances from outside. Further, since they resemble one another quite closely, they are presumed to anticipate one another's reactions quite accurately.

2.1.2 Formation of Strategic Groups

How do strategic groups form within an industry? Random initial differences, differences in firm goals and risk profiles and the historical evolution of industry, have been identified as factors contributing to the formation of strategic groups (Porter, 1979). Random initial differences in assets and skills ensures that some firms outdistance others in racing towards the strategic space which is maximally protected within an industry. Secondly, individual firms have different risk and time preferences and since investments in mobility barriers are risky (as discussed below), some firms are more prone to making such investments than others.

Finally, the historical evolution of industry such as changes in the market growth rate, can facilitate the formation of strategic groups. Industries which are characterized by high growth may provide an environment for firms to attempt different or innovative strategies with respect to production or product introduction. Capacity can be added profitably more often and in larger increments, thus allowing firms to adopt new production technologies more quickly. Also, early entry into certain industries provides some entrants with lower costs of adopting certain strategies than later entrants. On the flip side, the irreversibility of many forms of firm investment decisions precludes early entrants from adopting certain strategies pursued by later entrants, which capitalize on accumulated industry learning/wisdom. Thus the timing of entry is crucial.

2.1.3 Common Misconceptions about Strategic Groups

Let us now look at some of the common misconceptions concerning strategic groups. First, strategic groups are often confused with market segments (Harrigan,1985). This is a fallacy because strategic groups represent a whole approach to competing within a particular segment or arena and not just the choice of the arena. Additionally, while strategic groups signify heterogeneity on the supply side of the market, market segments represent heterogeneity on the demand side of the market (Cool 1985).

Second, Porter (1979), has warned against the misconception implicit in construing strategic groups as a redefinition of industry boundaries. Although oligopolistic interdependence is recognized more fully within groups than between them, it is also recognized more fully within industries than between them (Porter, 1976). Secondly, industry boundaries are delineated by identifying breaks in the cross elasticity of supply, and while group products are imperfect substitutes in marketing sense (by affecting conditions of sale), they are not imperfect substitutes in a physical sense.

Finally, strategic groups are not an extension of generic strategies. Generic strategies are more behavioral since they represent a strategic posture, while strategic groups are more structural and are a fundamental part of industry structure. Cool (1985: 109-110) notes: "Whereas generic strategy research postulates that there exist various types of strategies which are effective in different industrial settings, the strategic group concept is based on the premise that strategy formation is so industry-specific that it is *a priori* impossible to generalize across industries".

2.1.4 A Contemporary Definition of Strategic Groups

A strategic group is a relatively stable group of competitors that follow similar strategies along key strategic dimensions of industry. The nature of key strategic dimensions is industry specific depending on the fundamental industry structure and changes over time according to evolutionary forces (Ramsler 1982). Such evolutionary forces may include major innovations in product design or marketing methods that affect the current extent of product differentiation within the industry. Similarly, innovative breakthroughs in processing or transportation technologies, input components, or distribution capabilities can alter the various economies of scale or the absolute cost factors in the industry, thereby dramatically changing the competitive cost structures.

Additionally, changing demographic characteristics, income levels, or buyer tastes and requirements can affect the size of the current market or specific segments of the market. Change in government regulation or policies can rewrite the rules of the game in any competitive arena. Therefore, the elements of industry structure are forced to undergo continuous change by important evolutionary changes. Such change has a direct influence on the conduct of firms within the industry and on the nature of their competitive interaction.

Thus, strategic groups are a useful tool for dynamic modeling of industry evolution, in which firms with different strategies and different objectives make investments in improving their strategic position. Strategic group mapping can be a useful way of tracking industry dynamics as firms become more similar to or different from each other. "The matching of market segment changes with strategic group evolutions provides a useful means of predicting the nature of competition" (Harrigan, 1985). In this context then, strategic groups can help managers to focus their attention upon differences in how competitors approach the market place. It can help them to assess

-The attractiveness of market opportunities for their firm (and for their competitors);
-Their ability to exploit industry changes;
-And hence, their long term opportunities for profitability within the industry in question.

2.2 MOBILITY BARRIERS

Mobility barriers are at the heart of strategic groups theory. If strategic groups are present within an industry then there have to be mobility barriers in that industry and conversely if there are intraindustry barriers to changing strategic posture, the industry can be said to consist of strategic groups (Mcgee & Thomas, 1986). The concept of mobility barriers was first advanced by Caves & Porter (1977) wherein they argued that theory of entry "becomes much richer-yet remains determinate - when set forth as a general theory of the mobility of firms among segments of an industry, thus encompassing exit and inter-group shifts as well as entry" (Caves & Porter, 1977: 242).

In general, mobility barriers are structural or strategic barriers which surround a group and protect it from entry by potential rivals. Thus they provide a dual protection against entry by new competitors into the industry and from the threat of entry by incumbents in other groups moving into the group in question. But, these same protective barriers can act as traps or exit barriers, blocking either de novo exit from the industry or simply inter group movement. This was empirically demonstrated by Harrigan (1980) in her study of declining businesses and Mascarenhas & Aaker (1989) in their study of the oil drilling rig industry. The height of mobility barriers surrounding a group varies from group to group, with some groups enjoying protection of much stronger and higher barriers than others.

What factors give rise to mobility barriers? Joe Bain (1956) identified three sources of barriers in an industry in his general theory of entry. These are economies of scale, product differentiation, and capital requirements/absolute cost advantages of established firms. These standard sources of entry barriers can vary with the group and therefore translate into mobility barriers. For example, in a given industry some firms spend large sums of money on advertising and sales promotions to create a strong brand name for their products enabling them to charge premium prices, while others eschew such outlays and sell their products at low prices or unbranded.

Therefore, the extent of product differentiation often varies within an industry, and with it, the level of product-differentiation barriers to entry. Similarly, absolute cost barriers will be higher in the group of firms engaged in full-line production because of the greater capital outlay requirements and in groups defined by extensive vertical integration for the same reason. Again, because the groups' mixture of activities differ, their operative cost curves are not identical, and therefore, scale-economy barriers can vary among groups. In fact, scale-economy barriers provide an explanation for why entrants could rationally choose suboptimal scales when larger and lower cost sellers are present (Caves & Porter, 1977).

Mcgee (1985) and Mcgee & Thomas (1986) have identified three sources of mobility barriers: market related strategies which is akin to Bain's product differentiation, industry supply characteristics (the equivalent of Bain's economies of scale) and characteristics of the firm (an extension of Bain's absolute cost advantages and includes things like organization structure control systems and ownership). Twenty-one sources of mobility barriers are identified in Table 2.1. These are divided into three categories: economic (intrinsic), strategic and firm specific.

This classification, represents a comprehensive treatment of sources of mobility barriers. It should be noted that calculation of the height of these mobility barriers is still a "black art" (Shepherd, 1988) and moreover, it is not clear how these various sources combine, whether multiplicative or additive, to determine the height/strength of mobility barriers.

Investments in the creation of mobility barriers are risky in so far as the costs are irrevocable and change the overall cost make up of the group. While resale markets may exist for capital equipment and tangible assets, it is hard to recover differentiation costs or investments in R & D. Similarly, if the creation of mobility barriers increases the fixed cost component of the groups' overall costs then it increases the groups' susceptibility to changes the in environment (i.e., its riskiness).

A related notion is that there are significant costs associated with inter-group mobility along with a time lag. Oster (1982: 238) notes, " At the heart of the strategic groups theory is the idea that there are rigidities associated with change". This means that any strategic group scheme based on mobility barriers, should be relatively stable over time. If substantial mobility is observed between groups, then one can question the presence of mobility barriers and the validity of strategic groups, in absence of clear evidence of barrier lowering investments by firms. Excessive mobility then should be evidence that strategic groupings have not been identified (Mascarenhas & Aaker, 1989).

Mobility barriers represent for the group members an investment in a collective, sometimes intangible, capital asset whose benefits are shared between group members (Mcgee 1985). Firms' shares of the rents from this collectivity will probably be in proportion to their share of sales (Caves & Porter 1977). However, in absence of collusion, the level and design of these investments will be tailored by individual firms to yield them the maximum share of the incremental joint profit stream. This would then give rise to Hatten and Hatten's (1987) notion of asymmetrical mobility barriers. The challenge for strategists then is to create entry barriers into one's own group while reducing exit barriers, and to recognize that different barriers may be needed to keep out potential competitors from differentially positioned groups.

2.3 STRATEGIC GROUPS AND FIRM PERFORMANCE

Strategic groups are extremely useful for investigating intra industry profit differences. According to Porter (1979) "The concept of strategic groups allows us to systematically integrate differences in the skills and resources of an industry's member firms and their consequent strategic choices into a theory of profit determination."

In their early work, Caves and Porter (1977) focused exclusively on the performance consequences of strategic group membership. They emphasized entry barriers, collusion and market power at the group level and suggested a strong association between group membership and firm performance, with firms occupying groups protected by the highest mobility barriers enjoying superior performance. Porter (1979, 1980) in his later work, significantly shifted his focus from group level performance to firm level performance. He contended that consideration of market factors, as well as firm-specific factors, would enhance performance predications over those based on mobility barrier considerations alone.

While mobility barriers still occupied a central place in the determination of firm performance, Porter argued that differences of scale, risk profile, asset endowments and the ability to execute a chosen strategy among group members significantly moderated the linkages between mobility barriers and firm performance.

However, empirical research (Cool & Schendel 1987, Frazier & Howell 1983, Porter 1979, Dess & Davis 1984 among others) continued to focus on establishing across group performance differences and produced mixed results.

As pointed out by Cool & Schendel (1988), the huge within-groups variance of performance among group members might have dwarfed the between-groups variance and thus may account for inconsistent findings. This line of thinking focuses on capability management and isolating mechanisms at the firm level. It challenges the assumption that group members are very similar (i.e., incumbents equally share profits). Two empirical studies in this direction have come out with significant findings. Lawless, Wilsted & Bergh (1988) in their multi-industry study of 55 manufacturing firms broadly divided into two groups, find significant performance differences among firms within groups. This is attributed to differences in firm capabilities as shown by a significant correlation between firm capabilities and performance. Cool and Schendel (1988) in a study of the pharmaceutical industry divided the industry into 5 groups and found significant performance differences among group members within groups which were attributed to firms' risk profiles and accumulated asset endowments (broadly, firm capabilities or competencies).

Hence, strategists should bear in mind that simply being a member of the maximally protected group within an industry, or shifting to one, is no guarantee of superior performance. Unless a firm possesses deep firm-embodied skills to implement "superior" product market strategies and its asset base is aligned with its strategic posture, it will not be able to extract economic rents. However, if their is intense rivalry among the members of the dominant group, excessive profits would be competed away.

Summarizing, it may be said that an understanding of firm performance determinants is enriched by employing the strategic groups framework and that the strategic groups concept holds considerable promise for studying and predicting differential performance of industry members.

2.4 STRATEGIC GROUPS AND COMPETITIVE RIVALRY

Oligopoly theory predicts that collusion by oligopolists on restricting output or price fixing enables oligopolists to exercise market power - the ability to hold price above marginal cost, so that they can earn abnormal profits. Oligopolists may collude overtly or they may employ facilitating devices to collude tacitly and maximize joint profits. The more concentrated the market, the more standardized the product, the more comparable the costs and rates of time preference across firms, the more likely oligopolists are to reach an agreement (Stigler, 1964).

But the presence of heterogenous strategic groups complicates oligopolists agreement on a common set of market goals and reduces the degree of adherence to a tacit agreement. Additionally, while oligopolists as a group will always have an incentive to collude, oligopolists as individuals will always have an incentive to cheat on a collusive agreement (Stigler, 1964). The presence of divergent strategic groups with less common interaction via common customers, suppliers, and channels of distribution, restricts the mutual flow of information, thereby reducing the ability to rapidly detect cheating and hence undermining the stability of tacit agreement. Newman (1978 :418) notes, "If firm membership in different strategic groups can signal differences in their market goals and reflexes, it is clear that an industry with a more complex structure of strategic groups should (ceteris paribus) display more rivalrous conduct".

Porter (1979) has identified three factors which explain the intensity of rivalry within an industry: (i) the number and size distribution of groups, (ii) the degree of market interdependence and (iii) the strategic distance between groups. Discussion of each of these is organized around the following questions:

(1) How does the configuration of strategic groups influence rivalry ?

(2) How do changes in the make-up of strategic groups affect rivalry ?

(3) Are all strategic groups equally potent in influencing industry rivalry ?

(4) How is one group affected by rivalry with other groups ?

2.4.1 Configuration of Groups

The configuration of strategic groups consists of the number and size distribution of strategic groups within an industry (where size is equal to the aggregate market shares of group members), the market interdependence between groups - the extent to which different groups compete for the same customers, and the strategic distance - the degree of strategic asymmetry between groups. Where the industry consists of few groups of more or less equal size, the potential for rivalry in terms of price or non-price competition is much greater, therefore the chances of tacit collusion are much higher.

On the other hand, where the industry is populated by a large number of groups of unequal size, it is extremely difficult to work out any collusive agreement and much more difficult to enforce such a agreement. Moreover, it is anticipated that the greater the distance among strategic groups, the less their mutual interdependence, and more difficult will be any tacit collusion among them. Therefore, it is more likely that a strong rivalry will exist in such a industry.

Finally, market interdependence can work both ways. It may be expected that with a high level of interdependence, competition will not only be intense but also varied in form, reflecting the diverse asset structures of competitors. On the other hand, a high level of interdependence can force the rivals to come to the bargaining table and work out some kind of an agreement. The key seems to be the strategic distance and the relative sizes of the groups competing for the same market. Where there is a great diversity in the strategic postures of these interdependent groups of unequal sizes, the possibility of any tacit collusion is extremely remote and the rivalry should be at its fiercest, while less strategic distances among equal sized interdependent groups will help to tone down the degree of rivalry.

2.4.2 Changes in Group Membership

The make-up of strategic groups and changes in membership over time provides us a window into the historical patterns of competition within an industry. Essentially, analyzing membership forces the researcher to look at the specific structure of each group. Where groups are composed of unequal sized firms, scale differences work to the advantage of large firms when economies of scale or captive distribution arrangements are present (Porter,1979). Similarly, entry of a vertically integrated player from an adjacent industry could severely disrupt the stability of any existing agreement among group members or across groups, thereby leading to an increase in rivalry. This occurs because a vertically integrated producer can indirectly shade the cartel price (if there is an price agreement) if it in operates in downstream industries. A classic example is OPEC, where by integrating forward into refining and distribution, many OPEC nations have acquired the ability to cut the price of crude oil discreetly. Further, where the costs of mobility into the group differs among group members, their risk and time preferences are likely to vary, making it difficult to enforce any collusive agreement and therefore increasing competition within the groups.

2.4.3 Group Power

All strategic groups are not equally potent in influencing industry rivalry. The key is to focus on the most protected group or the one surrounded by highest mobility barriers (Porter,1979). In a sense, this is the dominant group in the industry. The firms within this group will fully recognize their interdependence and therefore, are likely to hold price while competing on other variables or investments in entry deterrence. This would then provide a 'price umbrella' for other groups, even though profits were competed away in the protected group. This 'price umbrella' while assuring superior profits for less protected groups (provided they control mutual rivalry), also shifts the overall pattern of competition within the industry.

2.4.4 Industry Rivalry

Finally, the effect of inter-group rivalry is dependent on the mobility barriers surrounding groups. The group with the higher barriers has a greater profit potential, if the competition within the group is not strong. But, the outbreak of competitive warfare in this group is likely to spill over into adjacent groups through market interdependence, forcing them to respond and thereby, competing away the profits of both the groups. Similarly, where one group enters into a new wage agreement with its labor unions, it is going to alter the cost structures of surrounding groups.

2.5 EMPIRICAL STUDIES

Early work (Newman 1978, Porter 1979, Caves & Pugel 1980, Oster 1982, Greening 1980, Hatten & Schendel 1977) following Hunt's (1972) research was chiefly concerned with identifying intra industry heterogeneity and establishing that firms in an industry differed in more important respects than just size. This was appropriate since, in effect, it amounted to proving that firm conduct could affect industry structure and consequently performance in important ways.

But, still strategic groups remained only a "sort of dynamized add on to the S-C-P paradigm" (Caves, 1984). Later work in this stream of research focused on testing the performance implications of the strategic group membership. However, the few empirical findings on this differential performance hypothesis are conflicting and extremely confusing.

The empirical work on stategic groups can be best classified by differentiating between the basis used for strategic group identification. Most studies have employed similarities in the observed strategic behavior or conduct of the firms to identify strategic groups within industries. This approach can be further broken down into bivariate classification schemes and multivariate classification schemes. The bivariate studies are conducted in spirit of original Harvard studies on groups (Hunt 1972, Newman 1973, Porter 1973) and use a much narrower operationalization of strategy. Groups are typically identified by using one or two (up to four) variables such as size, advertising intensity, vertical integration, R&D expenditures, geographic origin etc. These studies generally employ large, cross-sectional sampling frames encompassing several industries.

The multivariate studies are conducted in the spirit of the original Purdue studies on the Brewing industry (Schendel, Hatten & Cooper 1978; Hatten & Schendel 1977; Hatten, Schendel & Cooper 1978) and employ a much richer and broader operationalization of strategy. These are essentially single industry studies and use multiple strategic variables (marketing, finance, manufacturing, operations etc.), which capture the key bases of competition in the industry, to identify strategic groups.

The second approach to group identification is the use of mobility barriers. This is a relatively recent, but promising, approach.

The argument here is that since mobility barriers represent the theoretical core of the concept and deter movement between groups, they should be the relevant basis for group identification. Proponents of this approach argue that mobility barrier based groups provide a very different conceptual focus than a common strategy conceptualization of strategic groups because mobility barriers are resource dependent and are driven by firm assets and skills (Mascarenhas & Aaker 1989).

The last approach to group identification is the use of the capital asset pricing model of finance theory. In this approach, firms whose security returns are correlated are put into the same group. Although the idea is interesting, there is only one study (Ryans & Wittink 1985) of this type in the literature.

Table 2.2 provides a detailed summary of empirical strategic groups studies in terms of choice of variables, sample frame, data analytic method and findings. A comprehensive review of the strategic group literature is available in Cool (1985) and Mcgee & Thomas 1986).

2.6 UNSETTLED QUESTIONS

Despite this plethora of research which the strategic groups concept has spawned, three fundamental questions pertaining to this stream of research remain largely unsettled and are subject to considerable debate among the scholars in the field. (1) Are strategic groups an integral part of an industry structure or are they mere statistical artifacts? (2) What are the performance implications of strategic group membership? (3) How stable are these group structures over time? It is interesting to note that the first question concerning the definition/identification of the groups essentially drives the other two. In the following paragraphs, I elaborate on each of these issues.

2.6.1 Existence of Strategic Groups

The question of existence involves both methodological and conceptual issues. The standardized methodologies employed for discovering strategic groups in an industry such as clustering or other data reduction techniques are inherently biased in favor of uncovering clusters of data from a large data set. But this amounts to creating rather than discovering natural structures, since the underlying assumption is that these groupings do in fact exist (Barney & Hoskisson 1990).

In a review of 27 studies, Barney and Hoskisson (1990) found that all of them including the multi-industry studies of Harrigan (1980: 8 industries) and Hergert (1983: 50 industries), found the presence of strategic groups within industries. Barney and Hoskisson (1990:7) observe that "the development of clusters, per se, cannot be used as a test of the existence of strategic groups. In this analytic approach, strategic group theorists are left in the uncomfortable position of assuming that strategic groups exist, applying algorithms that are guaranteed to generate clusters, and then concluding that the obtained clusters demonstrate that strategic groups exist. The tautology here is obvious".

These empirical limitations however, do not negate the concept of strategic groups. On a conceptual level, it is important to develop a theory of strategic groups which will predict the presence, as well as the absence, of strategic groups, depending upon the conditions in the industry. Also, it is important to empirically establish the existence of strategic groups in as many industries as possible (Galbraith & Schendel, 1983). The validity of these groupings then needs to be confirmed with managers so as to determine whether the findings corroborate the perceived natural groupings in the industry.

2.6.2 Strategic Groups and Performance

The question of performance is directly linked with correct identification of strategic groups in the industry. It may be argued that the data driven nature of most strategic group studies has led to invalid identification of strategic groups, and consequently, has failed to unequivocally establish performance differences across groups. Another contributory factor may be the huge within groups variance, which would dwarf across group performance differences (Cool & Schendel 1988). Further, almost all studies, except the most recent ones, employed unitary measures of performance. These measures fail to capture the multifaceted nature of the performance construct (Fieganbaum & Thomas, 1990).

Despite all these moderating explanations, it is important to clearly establish the linkage between strategic groups and performance. Thomas and Venkatraman (1988: 541) note that "if strategic groups are to be truly useful for theory construction in strategic management, then there should be a relationship between strategic group membership and performance criteria".

2.6.3 Stability of Strategic Groups

Except for Oster (1982), Cool (1985), Fiegenbaum (1987), and Mascarenhas (1989), strategic group studies have not checked for the stability of derived groups over time. Most studies really have been snapshots in time. This is particularly worrisome, given the fact any claim of strategic groups being a fundamental part of industrial reality is unsubstantiated until the stability of these groupings is established. Further, along with temporal stability, the stability across variations in the dimensions used to develop the structure of strategic groups also needs to be established. For example, what would happen to the groups if we added or subtracted a strategy variable used for grouping analysis?

The above discussion highlights the ambiguous and equivocal nature of existing research regarding, the questions of existence, stability, and performance implications of the strategic groups. In conclusion, it may be said that we need a new way of thinking about the theoretical rationale for the existence of intraindustry heterogeneity and its attendant implications, so as to address the weaknesses of extant literature on the subject. A preliminary attempt is made towards this end by developing a resource/skill based model of strategic groups that draws on the emerging, resource based theory of the firm. The model calls for identifying strategic groups based on the accumulated asset endowments of the incumbents or the resource bundles employed to compete by the industry participants, rather than on the basis of their product market strategies.

2.7 AN ALTERNATIVE VIEW OF STRATEGIC GROUPS

Under the new realties of global competition, traditional strategic recipes no longer hold. Successful competitors build their strategies not around products but around deep knowledge of a few highly developed core skills (Hamel & Prahalad 1989). The management focuses on what it does best, avoids distractions, and leverages its organizational and financial resources far beyond what traditional strategies allow. Quinn et al (1990:60) argue that "now physical facilities - including a seemingly superior product - seldom provide a sustainable competitive edge. They are too easily bypassed, reverse engineered, cloned, or slightly surpassed. Instead, a maintainable advantage usually derives from outstanding depth in selected human skills, logistics capabilities, knowledge bases, or other service strengths that competitors cannot reproduce and that lead to greater demonstrable value for the customer".

As the above discussion illustrates, the underlying bases of competition have shifted from being more asset based to being more skill based. Therefore, any viable study of competitive patterns within an industry should concentrate on isolating underlying skills employed by firms to compete. Additional support for this line of thinking is provided by Mcgee and Thomas (1989: 105):

> "We maintain that among the set of distinctive assets in which a firm can invest are 'marketing' assets, i.e. *those abilities of the firm to perceive, interpret, and respond* to customer characteristics in such a way that rivals find it difficult and costly to replicate such behavior - thus, mobility barriers are created. In our view such barriers can be created in any sphere of the firm's operations. To discuss pricing (for example) on its own is less useful than examining how *distinctive firm-level characteristics (which are embodied in different asset structures)* influence competitive forces". (emphasis added)

These abilities and distinctive firm level characteristics which Mcgee and Thomas label as distinctive assets are what Aaker (1989) has termed as skills, defined as something that you do better than your competition. This label is more descriptive since these are intangible. These skills are the result of tangible underlying investments in assets, accumulated over a period of time.

The precise pattern of accumulation may vary from a firm to firm. A specific skill, then, is developed by a pattern of investments which a creates a distinctive asset structure or a skill. Of themselves, skills have no value both in input as well as output markets. Skills are firm specific and are acquired and nurtured over a long period of time with a deliberate strategic focus. Skills have an economic value only when they are employed with some combination of assets to implement chosen product market strategies.

A sample portfolio of skills may consist of knowledge about special product designs, advanced process technologies, innovative marketing and distribution methods, appropriate organizational structures, administrative procedures, etc. which the firm has acquired over a period of time. In any industry, successful players build their product market strategies around one or some combination of these skills.

The underlying competitive advantage, then, is provided by these skills, which also circumscribe the competitive flexibility of firms in terms of their ability to change their strategic postures. Also, while specific strategic postures might vary among a group of firms, it is possible that they will derive their underlying competitive strength from the same set of skills. For example, there might be a group of firms within an industry which compete in the marketplace based on their skills in efficient manufacturing or their marketing competencies etc.

Thus, it may be inferred that systematic differences exist between firms as a result of 'strategic' resource choices, i.e. decisions to invest in building skills which are often difficult and costly to imitate. These skills then constitute the primary source of competitive advantage. Competitive differentiation is sustained by deploying a combination of assets and skills, since as argued above skills deployed by themselves create no economic value.

The combination of assets and skills is called a resource bundle or resource mix. The larger the proportion of skills in this bundle/mix, the more complex, less imitable and consequently more valuable it is. This can be understood by using an analogy from the construction industry where a mixture of cement and sand is used to make a plaster which then is used to fortify the brick structure of houses. The higher the percentage of cement in the mixture the stronger the resulting building. The cement in this example is akin to skills while the sand is akin to assets in our model.

The resulting resource bundle, then, is at the heart of a firms' strategic capabilities and thrusts. These resource bundles are the drivers of successful product market strategies. While superior performing product market strategies are transparent to every player in the industry, what is not so readily apparent is the resource base required to successfully implement those strategies. Even if such insights are obtainable, considerable time lag is required to acquire and cultivate the desired resource mix. Effective competition then occurs not at level of observed product market strategies (which merely reflects transient competitive positioning), but at the level of acquisition/creation of suitable resource bundles.

Any derivation of strategic groups based only on observed product market strategies would fail to capture this underlying competitive reality. It is the complexity of underlying resource bundles which sustain the firms' competitive advantage and prevents effective imitation of its strategies. These resource mixes are akin to notions of uncertain imitability and isolating mechanisms (Lippman & Rumelt 1982, Nelson & Winter 1982) and provide effective means of identifying strategic groups. Support for this line of thinking is found in Mcgee & Thomas (1986: 154) who state that - " Rumelt's isolating mechanisms therefore provide a basis for identifying groups on the basis of similar clusters of isolating mechanisms on the grounds that they are the phenomena which make competitive positions stable and defensible, given the uncertainty arising from unexpected changes in the environment".

Strategic groups, therefore, may be defined as groups of firms which compete within an industry by deploying similar resource bundles. Focusing on the isolation of resource combinations of the firm rather than its identifiable product market strategic posture can be understood by borrowing from the Systems Theory concept of equifinality. Katz and Kahn (1978:30) describe equifinality as follows: "According to this principle, a system can reach the same final state from differing initial conditions and by a variety of paths". Projected to the strategy context, this notion implies that identical goal sets can be attained by different resource combinations. However, since some of the resource combinations are inherently more efficient than others, economic rents will accrue to firms employing superior combinations. This will then translate into performance differences between firms following similar strategies or "within groups variance". But if strategic groups are identified based on similarities in patterns of resource deployments rather than derived product market strategies, such confounding effects may not occur.

Table 2.1 Sources of mobility barriers

A) Economic (Intrinsic) causes of barriers.

1. Capital Requirements related to plant and firm size, and to capital intensity.

2. Economies of Scale (from both technical and pecuniary causes)

3. Product differentiation (occurring naturally among products)

4. Absolute Cost advantages (from many possible causes, including differential   wage rates)

5. Diversification (giving the possibility of massing and redeploying resources among branches)

6. Research and Development Intensity.

7. High Durability of Firm-Specific Capital (giving rise to sunk costs)

8. Vertical Integration (which may require entry to occur on two levels   at once).

B) Strategic Causes of Barriers:

1. Retaliation and Pre-emptive actions (by the use of price or other devices)

2. Excess Capacity (as a basis for effective retaliation or for threats of   retaliation)

3. Selling Expenses Including Advertising (to increase the degree of product differentiation)

4. Patents (which provide exclusive control over technology)

continued on next page

Table 2.1 continued

_____

5. Control over Other Strategic Resources (such as ores, locations, specific talents, etc.)

6. "Packing the Product Space" (in industries with high product differentiation, as in the US cereals industry)

C) Firm-Specific Factors:

1. Shared visions/culture.

2. Installed base of satisfied customers.

3. Reputation for Quality.

4. Customer Orientation/Services and Product Support.

5. Continuing Product Innovation.

_____

Adapted from Shepherd (1988).

Table 2.2 Empirical studies of strategic groups

Study	Industry	Basis for Group Formation	Data Analysis Method	Findings
Hunt (1972)	Home Appliances	Product line basis --degree of product diversification --differences in product differentiation --extent of vertical integration	Rule-of-thumb (ad-hoc)	Four strategic groups were identified; strong conduct differences across groups
Newman (1973, 1978)	34 four-digit consumer goods industries	Degree of vertical integration	Rule-of-thumb (ad-hoc); Multiple Regression Analysis	Six strategic groups were identified; performance differences exist across groups
Porter (1973, 1979)	38 three-digit consumer goods industries	Relative size of firm (sales) --leader/follower classification	Rule-of-thumb (ad-hoc); multiple regression analysis	Leader/follower classification was supported; weak statistical support for performance differences across groups
Caves and Pugel (1980)	73 U.S. manufacturing industries	Firm Asset Size	Rule-of-thumb; multiple regressional analysis	Small firms were more profitable in some industries. Reciprocal relationship between industry structure and firm conduct

Continued on next page

Table 2.2 (cont'd)

Study	Industry	Basis for Group Formation	Data Analysis Method	Findings
Hatten (1974), Hatten and Schendel (1977)	Brewing	Manufacturing variables --number, age, capital intensity of plants Marketing variables --number of brands, price and receivables /sales Structural variables --eight-firm concentration ratio --firm size	Regression analysis	Analysis supported the classification; successful strategies differed across groups
Harrigan (1980)	Declining industries: receiving tubes, synthetic soda ash, baby foods, acetylene, percolator, cigar, leather tanners, rayon	Multiple dimensions of strategic posture	Strategic space mapping	Groups conformed weakly to Porter's strategies. No consistent patterns of performance. Additional perceptual data were used to corroborate group classifications.
Dess and Davis (1984)	Paint and allied products	21 competitive strategy variables (reduced through analysis)	Factor and cluster analysis	Groups conformed weakly to Porter's strategies. No consistent patterns of performance. Additional perceptual data were used to corroborate group classification.
Oster (1982)	19 consumer goods industries	Product strategy: advertising to sales ratio	Multivariate statistical analysis	2 main groups (high/low) emerged; low levels of movement between groups

Continued on next page

Table 2.2 (cont'd)

Study	Industry	Basis for Group Formation	Data Analysis Method	Findings
Ramsler (1982)	Banking industry --100 largest non-US banks	Product market differentiation, size, geographic scope	Multivariate statistical analysis	Differences in strategic behavior with regard to market entry into U.S. were found; used groups to predict future strategic behavior
Lahti (1985)	Finnish knitwear industry	size, product-line	Rule-of-thumb (ad-hoc); 2 SLS	Sized based groupings were confused; performance differences across groups
Primeaux (1985)	Petroleum	size, investment behavior	Rule-of-thumb (ad-hoc); regression analysis	Three strategic groups based on size emerged; performance differences observed
Hawes and Crittenden (1984)	Supermarkets	Marketing strategy variables: (i) Target Market (ii) Product (iii) Provision (iv) Price (v) Buying (vi) Display	Multivariate statistical analysis	Four strategic groups emerged; similar to Miles and Snow's typology; performance difference across groups
Hatten and Hatten (1985)	Brewing	Marketing strategy variables: (i) Price (ii) Advertising (iii) Number of brands (iv) National relative market share	Regression analysis and space mapping	Useful extension of the initial Purdue studies to show the evolution of an industry over time

Continued on next page

Table 2.2 (cont'd)

Study	Industry	Basis for Group Formation	Data Analysis Method	Findings
Ryans and Wittink (1985)	Airline	Security price movements as reflective of similarities in strategies	Factor and cluster analysis	Unclear groupings; clear US trunk airline groups; more ill defined inter-national, regional, and intra-state groups
Hergert (1983)	2,450 SBUs representing 50 industries; broad sample of US manufactur-ing industry	Five variables --Advertising/sales --R&D/sales --Asset/Sales --Business unit sales/parent sales	Cluster Analysis	No clear pattern across industries. Most common number of clusters = 2; range from 2 to 6; performance differ-ences—equivocal
Frazier and Howell (1983)	Medical supply and equipment	Abell's (1980) three dimensions	MANOVA	Three groups emerged; no perform-ance differences; but conduct differ-ences across groups
Baird and Sudharshan (1983)	Office equip-ment and electronic computing industry	Financial strategy variables. --Leverage, current ratio, return on assets, dividend pay-ment ratio, times interest earned, size	Three Mode factor analysis	Six to eight strategic groups were found; conduct differences were identified across groups; patterns in group structure assessed over time
Hayes, Spence and Marks (1983)	Investment banking	Services offered by banks	Logit analysis	Four strategic groups emerged with strong competition within groups.

Continued on next page

Table 2.2 (cont'd)

Study	Industry	Basis for Group Formation	Data Analysis Method	Findings
Cool (1985)	Pharmaceutical	Range of variables reflecting scope and resource deployment	Cluster analysis	Performance differences exist across groups for the market share measure; no risk-adjusted differences; groups were relatively stable over time
Fiegenbaum (1987)	Insurance industry	Range of variables reflecting scope and resource deployment	Cluster and regression analysis	Stable group structures over time. Performance differences for same measures but not for risk-adjusted measures.
Mascareuhas (1989)	Oil-drilling	- Product diversity - Technological Capability - Global spread - Vertical Integration - Marketing orientation	Nonhierarchical Cluster Analysis	High degree of stability over time. Some changes in group strategy during economic growth and decline.
Mascarehas and Aakar (1989)	-do-	Mobility Barriers - Depth - Offshore - International	-do-	Groups should be identified using mobility barriers. Low barriers associated with high performance.
Lewis and Thomas (1990)	U.K. Retail Gocery	Three Different Methods Used - Size - Six strategy variables - Three performance based groups	- Cluster Analysis - Factor Analysis - Discussion Analysis	Within-group variation in performance dominates across-group variation.

Chapter III
Research Questions and Hypotheses

The lack of uniformity among various strategic group studies makes it difficult to bring a cumulative research perspective to this stream of literature (Thomas & Venkatraman, 1988). Despite the rich theoretical traditions from which strategic group theory emerged and the numerous empirical efforts to test its implications, three fundamental questions related to existence, stability and performance implications of strategic groups remain largely unresolved.

This study addresses some of these issues by examining two different models of stategic groups. In the first model, variables measuring scope and resource deployment strategies are used in a longitudinal analysis. The second model employs resource-based theory (Wernerfelt, 1984; Barney 1991). Measures of ten capabilities are obtained from an expert panel of investment analysts and are used in a cross-sectional investigation of industry heterogeneity. This analysis explores resource-based clusters as a means for specifying strategic groups and compares capabilities with positioning variables in accounting for intraindustry performance differences.

3.1 DYNAMIC CHARACTERISTICS OF STRATEGIC GROUPS

Q1.) *What are the dynamic patterns of strategic group formation and movement over a period of time? What is the impact of discontinuous environmental change on inter group mobility and firm level risk-return relationships?*

This question seeks to examine the stability of derived strategic groups and whether some groups are more stable than others. Investigation of the stability of identified groupings is fundamental to any strategic groups study because, as Mascarenhas and Aaker (1989) have pointed out, excessive mobility between groups indicates that meaningful groupings have not been identified. A dynamic perspective is employed to uncover whether changes in strategic group membership occur, and if so, what patterns can be observed in the membership changes.

Strategic group dynamics are associated with three different outcomes: a change in group strategy, a change in group membership, or a change in the number of groups (Mascarenhas, 1989). While the change in group strategy will be captured by the methodology employed to identify subperiods of strategic homogeneity, other types of changes will be tracked by constructing a summary index. This part of the research question does not lend itself to formal hypothesis testing, and therefore, a comparative-descriptive approach is employed.

In addition, the impact of environmental changes on inter-group mobility and risk-return relationships will also be studied. The intent here is to understand how discontinuous environmental change affects inter-group mobility (Mascarenhas 1989) and consequently, whether this produces negative risk- return functions as suggested by Cool and Schendel (1988).

H1:   *During periods of environmental discontinuity, there will be significantly greater inter-group mobility.*

Both adaptation theory and industrial organization economics suggest that environmental shifts drive strategy changes. According to the adaption perspective, organizations try to adapt to environmental changes (Meyer & Rowan, 1977) and IO economics holds that industry structure drives firms' conduct and performance (Bain, 1968). Rapid environmental changes, however, may result in misalignment between an organization and its environment, reducing the effectiveness of its current strategy and prompting changes intended to improve alignment (Miller & Friesen, 1986). Rumelt (1981) argues that unexpected events such as changes in technology, regulation, relative prices, and consumer tastes provide potential sources of rents and opportunities for strategic repositioning. Consistent with this, Mascarenhas (1989) in a study of the oil drilling industry found that periods of economic decline were associated with higher intra-industry mobility than periods of economic stability and growth.

H2:   *Environmental discontinuities will be associated with the observance of negative risk return relationships at the firm level.*

Conventional finance theory argues that there is a positive relationship between risk and return (Brearly & Myers 1971). However, high environmental uncertainty may force some firms to undertake strategies that do not turn out well, while the same events may provide other firms with opportunities that can be exploited at low risk relative to the potential return. This is so because firms have a differential ability to execute a chosen strategy due to differences in their resource endowments. In periods of rapid environmental change, these capability differences enable some firms to seize opportunities at low risk relative to return, while at the same time, causing other firms to take high risk actions relative to return (Cool & Schendel, 1988). Risk, therefore, is conceived in terms of lack of fit between current strategic behavior and accumulated resource base (Cool & Schendel, 1988). This gap may then induce the presence of negative risk/return relationships at the firm level. Bowman (1980, 1982) and Fiegenbaum and Thomas (1986, 1988) also found the presence of negative risk/return outcomes at the industry level.

3.2 PERFORMANCE IMPLICATIONS OF STRATEGIC GROUPS

Q2.) *What is the nature of the relationship between strategic group membership and firm performance?*

A central concern of strategic management is the pursuit of sustainable competitive advantage. Therefore, the investigation of the relationship between strategic group membership and performance forms a natural focus of this study. According to Lewis and Thomas (1990: 386), "Two theoretical possibilities may therefore be advanced in researching intra-industry performance differences. First, that there may be performance differences across groups but second, that the uniqueness of firm strategies directed to achieve distinctive sets of assets (capital, financial, human) may better predict within-industry performance differences".

Research question two then, seeks to examine whether some groups outperform other groups within the industry as predicted by strategic group theory (Caves & Porter, 1977). And, whether all members of the same strategic group realize similar levels of performance?

H3a: *Performance differences measured in economic terms will exist between strategic groups during stable strategic time periods.*

H3b: *Within each period of stable strategic group structure, strategic groups will exhibit different levels of risk.*

H3c: *Within each period of stable strategic group structure, strategic groups will exhibit dissimilar levels of risk-adjusted performance.*

Strategic group theory predicts that the presence of mobility barriers prevents the less successful players in an industry from imitating the strategies of their more successful rivals. This provides an explanation for persistent intraindustry performance differences (Caves & Porter 1977). Since the height of mobility barriers surrounding different strategic groups varies, stable performance differences are expected across groups. However, previous research on this issue is inconclusive. Porter (1979), comparing the performance of his "leader" and "follower" strategic groups, stated that leader groups outperform followers. However, the difference found was not statistically significant. Neither did Caves and Pugel (1980) find a difference in profitability between smaller and larger firms. Oster (1982), on the other hand, found that high advertisers outperformed low advertisers in those industries where advertising spending has lasting effects. Howell and Frazier (1983) found no difference in performance among their strategic groups in the medical supply and equipment industry, while Dess and Davis (1984) observed that their "generic" strategic groups in the paint and allied products industry differed on some performance measures while not on others.

More recently, Cool and Schendel (1987) found performance differences in terms of market share, but not in terms of profitability. In addition, risk and risk adjusted performance differences were not observed. Fiegenbaum & Thomas (1990) found performance differences only across economic and risk dimensions. Lewis and Thomas (1990) found support only for the return on sales measure of performance out of three measures employed to test differences across groups. Nevertheless, it is extremely important to establish the linkage of strategic groups to performance in order to determine the predictive validity and usefulness of the theory (Thomas & Venkatraman 1988, Fiegenbaum & Thomas 1990).

H4: *Firms belonging to the same strategic group will not realize similar performance levels.*

Cool and Schendel (1988) argued that a large within groups variation might have dwarfed the across group variation in performance. They found intra group performance differences among firms in their study of the pharmaceutical industry and suggested that these differences arose due to differential resource profiles of the group incumbents, which in turn led to differential ability to execute chosen strategies as suggested by Porter (1979). Lawless, Wilsted and Bergh (1990) found similar firm level effects in their multi-industry study. The burden suggested by these studies is that research examining the relationship between strategic groups and performance focus on within group differences, as well as between groups difference.

3.3 AN EXPANDED MODEL OF STRATEGY-PERFORMANCE LINKAGE

Q3.)   *Does the gap between capabilities and strategy account for the variation in measures of firm performance?*

According to the original strategic group theory as advanced by Porter (1979), strategic groups combine differences among an industry's member firms into a systematic theory of profit determination. Cool and Schendel (1988) in their study of the pharmaceutical industry, found significant performance and risk differences among firms within strategic groups. They attributed this to differences in firm asset stocks/capabilities. Even Porter (1979) suggested that differential ability to execute a chosen strategy may moderate the relationship between strategic group membership and firm performance. This research question seeks to test empirically whether variation in intra industry performance differences can be explained by incorporating both strategic group membership and firm capabilities into the predictive model.

H5:   *A model of intra industry performance difference that includes measures of firm capabilities together with strategic group membership as predictors will have more predictive validity (higher proportion of explained variance) than a model omitting capability measures.*

This hypothesis essentially seeks to test whether more variation in firm performance can be accounted for once firm capabilities are introduced in the model along with strategic group membership. If capability measures significantly increase the model's ability to account for performance variation, this would provide support for the arguments in Cool and Schendel (1988) and Porter (1979).

3.4 RESOURCE BASED STRATEGIC GROUPS

Q4.) *Are firm resource bundles better predictors of strategic group membership than observed product market strategies?*

As pointed out in the introduction, the term "strategic groups" was coined by Hunt (1972) to describe competition in the white goods industry . However, the pattern, nature, and intensity of competition has changed tremendously since then (Best, 1990).   While in the past competitive advantage has been derived from the creation of privileged product market positions, nowadays competitive advantage may accrue by investing in specialized skills and competencies that transcend products and markets (Hamel & Prahalad, 1989; Quinn et al 1990). These competencies in turn, may be the drivers of successful product market strategies. Effective competition therefore may occur at the level of creation of these competencies and rather than at the level of product market strategies (Prahalad & Hamel, 1990).

This research question, then, seeks to examine whether it is possible to capture competition at the competency level by mapping strategic groups? Further, if the analysis produces meaningful groups, then do these groups have better predictive validity in terms of differential performance effects than groups based on product market strategies.

H6: *Firm resource bundles can be employed to identify meaningful strategic groups, as measured by the assessments of industry observers.*

If competition in an industry really occurs at the level of resource accumulation and if these resources really drive product market strategies, then it should be possible to map groups of players in an industry who compete by deploying similar resource bundles. Both McGee and Thomas (1986, 1989) and Cool and Schendel (1988) have called for identifying strategic groups based on firm level distinctive competencies and accumulated assets, since these constitute the real source of competitive advantage. This exploratory hypothesis seeks to test whether empirical support can be found for this assertion. Further, following Barney and Hoskisson (1990:11) who argue that "without some independent test of a group structure's intuitive appeal, the use of intimate knowledge as a justification for choosing a particular group structure has limited scientific validity", the meaningfulness of derived groupings is corroborated by industry experts.

H7:   *Increased differential performance effects will be associated with resource based strategic groups, as compared to product market based groups.*

If these resource based groups are really more stable and well defined than the product market based groups as argued above, then we would expect to find strong   support for differential across group performance effects.

Chapter IV
Methodology

The setting for this study is the U.S. Banking industry. The banking industry has undergone tremendous changes in recent years brought upon by the forces of deregulation, technological developments, and globalization. These changes have provided much greater opportunities for competitive differentiation and have led to a significant increase in the degree of competition in this previously regulated and largely uniform industry.

The progressive deregulation of the banking industry in the last decade provides a fascinating insight into the dynamics of strategic readjustment as firms' with asymmetrical resource bases adopt different product market strategies to distance themselves from one another. This opportunity to observe the dynamic process of competitive reconfiguration by firms with differential resource profiles is the driving force behind the selection of this industry.

Two other considerations which influence the choice of the banking industry for the study are: (1) Detailed data bases are available for this industry. This facilitates a richer and more accurate description of industry specific strategies and strategic groups. (2) And, this researcher's own keen interest and working knowledge of this industry. An understanding of the industry is prerequisite for performing its strategic group analysis (Cool & Schendel, 1987).

4.1 RESEARCH DESIGN: LONGITUDINAL FACET

A two stage research design will be employed to test the above research questions and hypotheses. A longitudinal design will be used in the first stage to address research questions 1 and 2 and the accompanying hypotheses. Then in the second stage, a cross sectional design will be used to address research questions 3 and 4 along with their associated hypotheses. To enhance expositional clarity, the methodology for each of these stages is described separately.

4.1.1 Sample

The sample for this study is the top sixty firms in the U.S. Banking industry. Although there are some 12,000 banks in the United States, the top sixty banks capture approximately 65% of the aggregate banking assets. This sample limitation is imposed to facilitate detailed examination of intra-group performance patterns, firm mobility, and most importantly, identification of firm level competencies. A larger sample would make it almost impossible to execute the cross sectional facet of this study. (This is discussed below.) Further, all single industry, longitudinal studies of strategic groups have found it essential to impose limitations on their sample size, to enhance the depth and richness of analysis (Cool 1985; Fiegenbaum 1987).

The top sixty banks based on asset size were identified in 1988, and then any bank which in ranked in the top sixty in any of the previous fifteen years (to 1974) was added to the list. This yielded a sample of 73 banks. However, for five of these banks - Boatmen's Bancshares, European American Bancorp., First American Corp.-Tenn., First of America Bank, and Meridian Bancorp. data was not available for the entire fifteen year period, and consequently, these were dropped from the sample. This yielded a final sample of 68 bank holding companies.

4.1.2 Data Sources

The primary data base for this study is Standard and Poor's Bank Compustat tapes. This data base provides financial, statistical and market information on approximately 146 of the largest, publicly traded banks. (As discussed above only 68 of these will be analyzed.) Data reliability and validity procedures are fairly rigorous. This data base was supplemented by Value Line Investor's Survey, 10-k annual statements, federal reserve bulletins, and the trade press.

4.1.3 Mapping the Strategic Space

Fiegenbaum and Thomas (1990) have suggested that any strategic group study should begin with a mapping of strategic space. Strategic space consists of the levels of organizational strategy, the components of strategic decisions and the chosen time period. An important initial step consists of the definition of the temporal horizon. . The time period chosen for this study is the period from 1974 to 1988. This fifteen year period covers six years before and eight years after the . passage of landmark Depository Institutions Deregulation and Monetary Control Act (DIDMA) of 1980 which significantly deregulated the industry. This, then would enable us to study the patterns of competition, both before and after deregulation in the industry.

The next step consists of resolving the issue of level of organizational strategy to be investigated. Following Fiegenbaum and Thomas (1990), it was decided to from groups at corporate strategy level since diversification in this industry occurs within the industry and not across industry boundaries. Also because of substantial tax advantages banks are structured in the bank holding company (BHC) form of organization. About 1800 of these BHCs or about 80% of the total consist of single banks, and the rest have a portfolio of 10-15 banks on average. Effective competition in the banking industry occurs at the level of these BHCs (Grady & Spencer, 1990).

The final step in mapping strategic space consists of identification of firms' strategies. Cool and Schendel (1987), and Hofer and Schendel (1978) have argued that scope and resource deployment components of strategy reflect major strategic decisions for a firm and that competitive advantage and synergy accrue as a result of these decisions. Therefore, it was decided to study the scope and resource deployment components of strategic decisions in the Banking industry.

Eleven variables reflecting these components were identified after a through literature search and discussions with industry analysts and executives. While an argument can be made that these variables are idiosyncratic and industry specific, this problem is unavoidable in strategic group research. The very nature of this line of inquiry is industry specific and requires a priori understanding of the industry by the researcher (Cool, 1985; Cool & Schendel, 1988). With that caveat in mind, this researcher believes that these variables adequately capture the key bases of competition in the banking industry. These were subsequently corroborated by the industry analysts who were interviewed for the cross-sectional phase of this study. Table 4.1 summarizes the definitions of these variables.

4.1.4 Strategic Variables

A) STRATEGIC SCOPE VARIABLES.

Scope commitments in the U.S. banking industry can be measured by product scope, geographic scope and product diversity.

1) *Product scope (CI, RE, TIM & DEM):* This is captured by four variables - the ratio of commercial and industrial loans to total loans (CI), the ratio of real estate loans to total loans (RE), the ratio of time deposits to total deposits (TIM), and the ratio of demand deposits to total deposits (DEM). CI is negatively correlated with consumer lending and represents the degree of involvement of the BHC in the wholesale market as opposed to retail market. RE[1] on the other hand captures the dependence of the organization on the specialized real estate market segment. TIM and DEM capture the stickiness and composition of a bank's funding base.

2) *Geographical reach (FND):* Since the domestic geographical scope of BHCs is restricted by the legal limitations on interstate/interregional banking in the U.S.,[2] the international reach of these BHCs is investigated by looking at the ratio of foreign owned deposits to the total deposit base. This variable is positively correlated with loans to foreign governments and interest rate swaps.

3) *Product diversity (NIR):* The percentage of noninterest revenues to total revenues is employed as a broad reflection of product diversity in the banks' strategy. This variable is a proxy for investment banking/fee based activities and in effect shows the extent of non traditional banking operations employed to generate revenues.

B) RESOURCE DEPLOYMENT VARIABLES.

Operations and finance are two key functional areas from which competitive advantage may particularly accrue to a banking organization. Indeed, control of expenses and loan loss reserves reflect operational efficiency, whereas the degree of leverage, funding strategies and investment decisions indicates differences in strategic financial skills. Five measures of resource commitments were developed in order to reflect these bases for establishing competitive advantage in the banking industry.

1) *Funding (NPF):* This is the ratio of net purchased funds to total assets. This ratio is negatively correlated with core deposits and liquidity and shows the degree to which the bank relies on purchasing funds in the open market rather than depending on its deposit base to

fund its assets. In effect the higher this ratio is, the more aggressive the bank in its outlook and the more willing it is to make use of opportunities in the market place as they arise.

2) *Capitalization (LEV):* This ratio captures the degree of financial leverage or the riskiness of the banks' strategy. It is operationalized as the ratio of equity capital to total assets.

3) *Investments (GRA):* For a bank, the investment decisions basically consist of finding ways to increase its asset base. The U.S. banking industry has seen a spate of intra-state and intra-regional mergers and acquisitions of smaller banks by the larger BHCs since the process of deregulation was set in motion in the early 80s. This activity is captured by looking at the year to year growth in assets.

4) *Expense ratio (CS):* This is a measure of efficiency and shows the degree to which the banking organizations focus on keeping costs down in their production process in order to establish a competitive advantage. It is operationalized as the ratio of non- interest expenses/total assets.

5) *Provisions (PROV):* This is the percentage of loan lease loss reserve/average loans and leases and reflects the efficiency and effectiveness of a bank's production process in recognizing problem loans and making adequate provisions against those losses.

4.1.5 Performance Variables

The performance of firms is a complex and a multidimensional phenomenon. Recently, accounting based measures of performance have been subject to criticism (Fisher & McGovern, 1983; McGuire & Schneeweis, 1983). Some of the problems cited include: accounting manipulation, undervaluation of assets, distortions due to depreciation policies, inventory valuation, treatment of certain revenue and expenditure items, and differences in the methods of consolidating accounts. A distinction is also generally drawn between economic performance (which presents a static picture grounded in historical trends) and strategic performance (which looks at the future value/earning power of the firm). Freeman (1984), for example, has noted that the usual focus on economic goals is too myopic in the context of strategic management. He suggests that strategic management actions should be evaluated according to their impact on the broad set of stakeholders, rather just shareholders.

In this study I employ strategic measures of performance instead of economic measures to capture the performance construct more meaningfully. Chakarvarthy (1986: 437) argues that " useful measures of strategic performance are those that help assess the quality of a firm's adaptation." He further suggests that firm adaptation is critically dependent on the generation of slack resources. He notes that "profitability, productivity and the ability to raise long-term resources form the core measures in the study of slack resources available to a firm" (Chakarvarthy 1986: 450). Three different performance variables, therefore, are employed along each of these dimensions. These are:

1) *ROAA:* This is the standard return on average asset measure frequently employed to evaluate bank performance. This measures the profitability aspect of strategic performance.

2) *Employee productivity (PPE):* For a service organization like a bank, human resources are its biggest resource, and therefore productivity per employee is an important performance criteria. This is operationalized by dividing the net profit by the number of employees. This then measures the productivity aspect of strategic performance.

3) *P/E Ratio:* Price earnings multiple is a market based measure of performance and reflects the price multiple/premium which the financial markets are willing to pay over firms' current earnings. In essence, this is a measure of discounted flows of the firms' estimated future earnings and reflects its future earning power. It reflects the third dimension of strategic performance, namely the ability to raise long term resources.

4.1.6 Risk Measures

Risk will be measured by estimating the variance of returns within each strategic period for each measure of performance. Many researchers have used the variance of a firm's return over time as a proxy for risk (Armour & Teece, 1978; Bettis, 1981; Bettis & Hall, 1982; Bowman, 1980; Christensen & Montgomery, 1981; Fisher & Hall, 1969; Rumelt, 1974). Finally, risk-adjusted measures will be calculated by simply dividing the strategic performance by their risk estimates. In sum, this procedure will give us nine measures of performance. Table 4.2 presents an overview of these measures.

4.1.7 Identification of Stable Strategic Time Periods (SSTPs)

The structure of strategic groups may change over time as firms alter their strategic mix in order to match their skills and resources to the opportunities and threats in the external environment. Consequently, it is important to identify subperiods of homogeneity for which strategic group structure is more stable within each period than between periods. Fiegenbaum & Thomas (1990) have suggested that SSTPs should be identified by using the following criteria:

    (1)   The variance-covariance matrix of the strategic variables should remain unchanged.

    (2)   The average (mean) behavior of the firms in terms of the strategic variables should remain relatively unchanged.

The rationale for using first criteria is that when firms change commitments along the strategic variables, the covariances between these variables should reflect this strategic repositioning. By determining the point in time when the covariance structure for all firms considered simultaneously, changes from previous periods, it is possible to establish breakpoints where significant dissimilarities occur. These breakpoints indicate the existence of distinct subperiods with different strategic group structures (Cool 1985).

The rationale for the second criteria is that it is possible for values of the strategic variables to change without changing the value of the variance-covariance matrix. In this case, although the relative relationship between strategic variables will remain the same, the entire industry will have shifted to a new set of mean values in terms of key strategic decision variables. Therefore, Fiegenbaum and Thomas (1990) recommend that SSTPs should be identified by looking at changes in both mean vectors and variance-covariance matrices.

The procedure to evaluate SSTPs over t time periods starts by testing the hypothesis of equality of the covariance matrices for first two periods.

$$H_0 : \Sigma_1 = \Sigma_2$$

against H_1 : both are not equal

where Σ represents the variance/covariance matrix between strategic variables for a specific period.

If the null hypothesis of no change between the two periods is accepted for a chosen significance level, then the two periods are pooled and the third period is introduced as

$$H_0 : \Sigma_{12} = \Sigma_3$$
$$H_0 : \Sigma_1 = \Sigma_{23}$$

against H_1 : not all Σ are equal (for both H_0)

where Σ_{12} and Σ_{23} denote the variance-covariance matrices of data pooled over the first two periods and the last two periods.

Two null hypothesis are tested because even if the variance-covariance matrix for first two periods is not significantly different form the last period, significant change might occur over the last two periods. If both null hypothesis are accepted, then the three periods are pooled together and procedure continues. In general, the following test procedure is performed in year i:

$$H_0 : \Sigma_{12} - - - - - - - - - - \text{-i-1} = \Sigma_i$$
$$H_0 : \Sigma_{12} - - - - - - - - - - \text{-i-2} = \Sigma_{i\text{-}1i}$$

$$H_0 : \Sigma_1 = \Sigma_{23} - - - - - - - i$$

against H_1 : Not all Σ are equal

A similar procedure is performed for the mean vectors. To verify the statistical significance of the changes, Bartlett test (Green 1978) will be used to test the equivalence of two sets of variance/covariance matrices, while Hotelling's T^2 test (Green 1978) will be used to compare two sets of means.

4.1.8 Analysis

Strategic groups will be identified by using a cluster analysis. A good clustering algorithm groups cases into clusters, maximizing the across cluster variation, while simultaneously minimizing the within cluster variation, so as to yield a tight clustering solution. Previous research has used hierarchical agglomerative clustering techniques to identify strategic groups. However, these techniques are biased in favor of generating equal sized clusters, and they suffer from the centroid drift problem (Punj & Stewart, 1983). Therefore, this study will employ a more sophisticated two stage clustering algorithm, where hierarchical clustering technique (Ward's minimum variance criterion) will be used in the first stage to arrive at the seed values and approximate number of clusters for subsequent iterative partitioning in the second stage.

The following stopping rule recommended by Harrigan (1985) and Fiegenbaum & Thomas (1990) will be used to determine the optimum number of clusters in each SSTP:

1) An additional cluster increases the overall fit (measured in terms of R^2 coefficient) by less than 5 percent ($R^2 \backslash < 5\%$).

2) The clusters obtained explains at least X% (X to be determined empirically by the nature of the data) of the overall variance ($R^2 >/ X\%$).

A multivariate analysis of variance (MANOVA) will then be performed across strategic groups to establish whether identified clusters really have different profiles of strategic scope and resource deployment commitments. Then a one-way analysis of variance (ANOVA) will be performed on every strategic variable, for each period, to determine on what competitive dimensions the identified strategic groups really differ.

Again MANOVA and ANOVA tests, using performance measures as dependent variables and strategic group membership as independent variables, will be performed across and within groups in each SSTP to test the associations between strategic groups and performance (H3) and to examine within groups performance variance (H4). The impact of discontinuous environmental changes on inter-group mobility (H1) will be examined by constructing a mobility index. Finally, the presence of negative risk return relationships (H2) will be tested by performing a regression of return on risk.

Summarizing, this facet of analysis will begin by mapping out the strategic space and then identifying sub-periods of strategic homogeneity (SSTPs) within the study period. Strategic groups will be identified within each of these SSTPs by performing a two-stage cluster analysis. Statistical techniques of regression analysis, MANOVA, and ANOVA will then be used to test hypothesis H2 through H4.

4.2 RESEARCH DESIGN: CROSS-SECTIONAL FACET

In the second stage of this study a cross-sectional research design is employed to address research question numbers three and four and test hypotheses five, six, and seven. This part of the project is field based and involves formulation of an expert panel. This expert panel will be composed of bank analysts at major investment houses. Analysts have been recognized to be the best and most authoritative sources for industry information (Brown & Rozoff 1983).

4.2.1 Composition of the Expert Panel

Three criteria were established to pick bank analysts for the panel of industry experts:
- Each individual should have at least ten years experience in the industry.
- He/She should be frequently quoted and interviewed in the *Wall Street Journal* and the business and trade press.
- They should be working for a major Wall Street investment bank.

Following these criteria, a ten person panel was constituted. Table 4.3 lists the names and affiliations of panel members at the time of data collection. This panel cumulatively embodies over 200 years of industry experience and represents the "creme-de-la-creme" of the industry.

4.2.2 Data Collection

This process began in the summer of 1991 with an initial round of interviews with Hanley, Bryan, Aspinwall and Dempsey. It is worthwhile to note that Hanley and Bryan are widely regarded as one of the best analysts' and consultants' respectively, in the industry. While both Aspinwall and Bryan have written internationally recognized books on banking strategy.

At these preliminary interviews discussions focused on understanding the key drivers of competition in the banking industry. Professor Ingo Walter (1986), who is an acknowledged authority on the banking industry, has identified a set of eight key capabilities/skills which provide competitive advantage in the financial services industry. This list was utilized to provide a framework for these discussions. Based on the input from these experts the initial list of eight was expanded and recast into ten key resources which provide a sustainable competitive advantage in the banking industry. These are detailed below at end of this subsection.

Another issue which came up for discussion at these initial interviews was nature and design of the instrument for measuring these resources. I wanted to employ questionnaires with industry grounded anchors, but it was suggested that this was not feasible (for instance, it is very difficult to operationalize placing power from high to low), and unnecessary, since these people were experts. Consequently, single rating sheets were developed which measured each of the ten resources on a seven point Likert scale ranging from low to high. Appendix I shows a sample rating sheet.

In the next stage, each of the panel members was personally contacted for semi-structured interviews. These discussions began by a general discussion of competitive dynamics in the industry. This served as an ice-breaker and a credibility builder. Then an overview of the entire study was presented to them, and finally, the importance and relevance of each of the ten resources was discussed to establish a common frame of reference. After the panelists understood the study, they were asked to rate the banks that they personally followed on each of the ten resources. One rating sheet was used for each bank and these rating sheets along with written description of the ten key resources was left with the panel members, to be scored at their convenience and returned to this researcher.

To avoid potential perceptual biases, the panelists were asked to rate each bank with respect to the industry as a whole and not with reference to the group that they followed[3]. While a certain degree of contamination by the "halo effect" (superior performers being rated high on every thing) is unavoidable, all references to performance were scrupulously avoided during the interviews and in the description of capabilities. This strategy did seem to work, as some poor performing banks (Marine Midland, Republic NY) were rated highly, indicating their long term value, while current high performers (e.g.Boatmen's bancshares) were rated poorly, indicating its poor strategic health.

4.2.3 Sample

It is important to note that most analysts follow 15-20 banks on an average and most investment banks generally track the top 25-30 banks. This places a limitation on the sample for which data could be collected from the expert panel. But it does increase the reliability and validity of the measures. It was decided to get a minimum of three ratings for each bank. Also, for some larger firms like Goldman Sachs and Kidder Peabody, two or three different analysts rated the banks that they personally followed, thereby increasing the reliability of the data. Following this procedure a final sample of 44 banks was assembled, each rated by at least 3 analysts. On about 30 banks, more than five different ratings were obtained. All of these banks fell within the top sixty ranked by asset size as of March 31, 1991. A high degree (.88) of inter-rater reliability was evident.

Next, I elaborate on definitions of the ten resources for which data was collected. These are ranked in descending order of importance, as suggested by Mr. Hanley of Saloman Brothers. The discussion here closely follows Walter (1986).

4.2.4 Description of Key Resources

1) *Management Quality and Depth:* The quality and depth of a banks' management team is the most critical resource in establishing a sustainable competitive advantage. In some sense, it is the most generic of all skills from which the others flow. The quality of leadership, clear strategic vision, management development, ability to attract and retain high quality people, compensation and reward systems, and prevalence of a credit culture determine the quality and depth of management.

2) *Franchise:* According to Walter (1986:38) "an institution's franchise is its most intangible asset, yet one that clearly distinguishes ex post the most successful competitors --- from the rest". Strategic management research is also paying increasing attention to corporate reputations as a source of competitive advantage. A banks' franchise is generally linked to a specific type of competence and expertise, developed over time and valued by the market.

3) *Asset/Credit Quality:* Banks fund their assets (primarily loans) by their deposit base and by purchasing funds in the open market. In the deregulated banking environment, firms are increasingly forced to bid for funds. The perceived quality of the firms' asset base reflects the riskiness of its loan portfolio and is an determinant of its funding cost. This is particularly evident in the interbank market where institutions with lesser perceived quality or riskier asset structures are forced to pay a premium over other firms in order to fund themselves. This premium also signals an impaired credit rating to the banks' clients, further damaging its competitive position. The perceived quality of institutional

risk base thus conveys substantial advantages on the funding side and sends strong signals to corporate clients.

4) *Technological Expertise:* Technological systems and capabilities provide tremendous advantage in the banking industry. Since banking is a highly knowledge intensive industry, the ability of the bank's technological systems to sift through large amounts of data and provide quality information on a real time basis is a valuable asset in the banking industry. Technology is both process and product related. Provision of decision support systems and "back office" processing systems represent the process aspect of technology in the banking industry. While financial engineering products such as corporate financial services, swaps etc. which generate fee based income for the bank, represent product related financial technologies.

5) *Placing Power:* This represents the distribution capabilities and "muscle" of a bank. With the continued securitization in the financial markets, placing power is becoming an increasingly important competitive variable in the banking industry. Placing power is very important for the investment banking arm of the banks in helping it to sell loans and arrange syndication.

6) *Adequacy of the Capital Base:* A strong capital base confers significant competitive power in the banking industry. It is the principal determinant of an institution's risk bearing ability and enables successful players to fully exploit market opportunities by engaging in mergers and acquisitions. Further, it facilitates introduction of specific products to the international markets and the provision of value added services to the clients. And finally, while it helps in achieving regulatory compliance, it also reduces the cost of funding.

7) *Resource Management/Efficiency:* This represents the ability of a bank to judiciously manage its physical and human resources so as to lower its fixed cost base, while obtaining high quality service from its human resources. Modern relationship based banking is essentially a "people business" and human resources are the single most critical competitive resource for service organizations, consequently their effective management is very important.

8) *Innovation:* In the banking industry innovation can be looked upon as the introduction of new process or technique that provides durable returns and adds significant value to the client. Due to the absence of any patent or copyright protection, the imitation-lag for financial innovations tends to be relatively short. Consequently, "it is important

for an institution to maintain a continuous stream of innovations - in this sense, an institution's most important innovation is its <u>next</u> one" (Walter 1986:37). While innovative capabilities are a function of the quality of human capital and technological expertise, they are also sensitive to organizational culture, management, reward systems, horizontal communication and cross-functional information exchange.
9) *Risk Management:* This represents the ability of a bank to prudently manage and evaluate its portfolio risk composed of credit risk, interest rate risk, default risk, exchange rate risk, along with its operating risk on an ongoing basis.
10) *Information Asymmetries:* Banking in particular and financial services in general is a highly information-intensive business. All forms of lending, development of client specific services and other credit related activities are critically dependent on the collection, processing and evaluation of large amounts of information. Information is unique, in that it is the only resource which can be used simultaneously in the production of a large number of services. In fact in 1984, Walter Wriston, former C.E.O. of Citicorp redefined Citicorp's business from banking to that of processing and selling information. Walter (1986:32) notes, "Indeed asymmetries of information among various competitors and their clients contribute a great deal toward explaining differentials in competitive performance".

The fact that there was lot of variance on the ratings (in other words, every bank was not uniformly excellent on all the ten attributes), and that a high degree of consensus was observed among the raters inspires confidence in the reliability of the procedure.

4.2.5 Analysis

Scores of each bank on these capability measures will be averaged and then used to cluster them into strategic groups. Same clustering procedure and stopping rules will be used as outlined in the analysis section of the longitudinal design. The resulting clusters will then be examined for validity. If these clusters are meaningful (as judged by the experts), then hypothesis six would be upheld. Hypothesis seven would be tested by performing ANOVA tests on performance measures for these clusters/groups, to determine if clear cut performance differences exist across these resource based strategic groups. The third research question and its accompanying hypotheses five, will be tested by using a variance decomposition model to partition intragroup performance differences into effects due to strategic group membership and effects due to firm capabilities.

Table 4.1 Corporate strategy variables and their definition in the
Banking industry

Strategic Component	Strategic Function	Strategic Variable	Definition
A. Scope	A1: Product scope	1. CI	$\dfrac{\text{Commericial \& Ind. loans}}{\text{Gross Loans}}$
		2. RE	$\dfrac{\text{Real estate loans}}{\text{Gross Loans}}$
		3. TIM	$\dfrac{\text{Total time deposits}}{\text{Total deposits}}$
		4. DEM	$\dfrac{\text{Total demand deposits}}{\text{Total deposits}}$
	A2: Geographic reach	5. FND	$\dfrac{\text{Foreign owned deposits}}{\text{Total deposits}}$
	A3: Product diversity	6. NIR	$\dfrac{\text{Noninterest revenues}}{\text{Total revenues}}$
B. Resource Deployment	B1: Production	7. C.S.	$\dfrac{\text{Noninterest expense}}{\text{Total assets}}$
		8. PROV	$\dfrac{\text{Loan-lease loss reserve}}{\text{Average loans \& losses}}$
	B2: Finance	9. NPF	$\dfrac{\text{Net purchased funds}}{\text{Total assets}}$
		10. LEV	$\dfrac{\text{Common Equity}}{\text{Total assets}}$
	B3: Investment	11.GRA	Year-to-year growth in assets

Table 4.2 Performance variables

Performance dimension	Performance measure	Notation	Definition
1. Economic	Return on assets	ROAA	Net Income -------------- Average Assets
	Price earnings ratio	PE	Closing Market Price -------------------- Earnings Per Share
	Productivity per employee	PPE	Net Income ------------------- Number of Employees
2. Risk	Risk of return on assets	SROAA	Standard deviation of ROAA
	Risk of PE mutliples	SPE	Standard deviation of PE
	Risk of productivity	SPPE	Standard deviation of PPE
3. Risk Adjusted	Risk-adjusted for ROAA	VROAA	The ratio of ROAA/SROAA
	Risk-adjusted for PE	VPE	The ratio of PE/SPE
	Risk-adjusted for PPE	VPPE	The ratio of PPE/SPPE

Note: Net Income is income before adjustments for extraordinary gains and losses.

Table 4.3 Expert Panel

- Thomas Hanley	Managing Director, Soloman Brothers
- Jim McDermott	President & Director of Research, Keefe Bruyette & Woods
- Judah Kraushaar	First Vice President, Merrill Lynch
- Charles Peabody	Sr. V.P. Research, Kidder Peabody
- Ted Paluszek	V.P. Research, Kidder Peabody
- Sally P. Davis	V.P. Investment Research, Goldman Sachs
- Tom McCandless	V.P. Investment Research, Goldman Sachs
- Dick Goleniewski	V.P. Investment Research, Goldman Sachs
- Michael Plodwick	V.P. Research, C.J. Lawrence Inc.
- James Hansbury	V.P. Research, Wertheim Schroder & Co.
- Frank Suoozo	V.P. Research, S.G. Warburg
- Ray Soifer	Manager, Brown Brothers Harriman

In addition, the following people contributed actively towards developing and refining the capabilities measure:

- Lowell Bryan	Managing Director & Chief banking Consultant, Mckinsey & Co.
- Dick Aspinwall	Chief Economist, Chase Manhattan
- Joe Dempsey	V.P. Manufactures Hanover
- Steve Rhoades	Chief, Financial Structure Div. Federal Reserve, Washington

Notes

1. To be more precise, the real estate portfolio should be broken down into commercial real estate and domestic real estate lending. Unfortunately, the compustat database does not provide such a breaksown, and therefore aggregate numbers were used.

2. Although restrictions on interstate banking have recently been removed, they were largely in place at the time of this study.

3. I am indebted to Professor Charles Fombrum for pointing this out to me.

Chapter V
Empirical Results

This chapter reports on the results of the analyses of the four research questions and their seven associated hypotheses in the U.S. Banking industry from 1974-1988. It begins by detailing the identification of sub-periods within the fifteen year study horizon and the mapping of strategic groups in each of these sub-periods. Then the results of individual hypotheses are presented.

5.1 IDENTIFICATION OF SSTP'S

The identification of stable strategic time periods (SSTP's) is the starting point of empirical analysis and is of critical importance. Since strategic groups will be mapped in each of these sub-periods separately, this procedure must be executed carefully.

As discussed in chapter four, the rationale for identifying subperiods is to uncover distinct periods in which the industry is more stable within a particular period than it is between periods. Fiegenbaum and Thomas (1990) have suggested two statistical tests to identify these points of transition:

1) To look at breaks in variance covariance matrices of strategic variables, using the Bartlett's F test.
2) To examine the shifts in mean vectors using the Hotelling's T-test.

To perform these tests, matrices consisting of data on the scope and resource deployment variables for each firm for each year were created. Then a iterative procedure as discussed in chapter three was employed to execute these tests. The process begins by comparing the variance covariance matrices and mean vectors of 1974 with 1975. If no differences are found then these two years are pooled and compared with 1976. Next, 1974 is compared with pooled 1975 and 1976, since even if no changes occurred in first two years, it is possible that some change might have occurred in the last two years. If both lead to a failure to reject the null hypothesis of no differences, then 1974, 1975 and 1976 are pooled. Iterative tests are conducted in a similar fashion up to 1988 according to the algorithm specified in chapter three.

The outcome of this test procedure depends upon the choice of the set of variables, the composition of sample firms, and the choice of the significance level defined for the statistical test (type-I error). To increase the robustness of results, a significance level of 1% (=0.01) was consistently applied across tests. Sensitivity analysis using jackknifing procedures were conducted by performing the statistical tests on a reduced set of variables and then on a reduced set of firms. This led to a total of 293 tests being conducted.

Table 5.1 shows the net result of these analysis. Hotelling's T test was found to be significant almost every year, indicating an increase in the magnitude of values on the scope and resource deployment variables. Since this did not correspond with actual industry events, and given the fact that mean vectors can shift due to effects of inflation, Hotelling's T test was deemed unreliable and exclusive reliance was placed on variance-covariance testing, for which a Box's M test (Neter & Wasserman, 1985) was employed. Cool (1985) and Cool & Schendel (1987, 1988) also relied exclusively on variance covariance testing to identify temporal breakpoints.

Statistical tests alone cannot guarantee that true "state of nature" has been discovered. However, corroboration of these results by significant industry events, can enhance the validity of these results. Table 5.1 compares the statistically derived SSTPs with industry events. The first transition occurred in year 1980 when the landmark DIDMCA was passed. The next break in 1983 followed the passage of another regulatory initiative the Garn St. Germain Act which further deregulated the industry. The 1986 and 1987 transitions represent the effect on the industry of the Mexican debt rescheduling and the LDC debt crisis. The 1988 subperiod shows a rebounding industry helped along by an overheated economy.

To ascertain how banks have repositioned themselves vis-a-vis each other, cluster analysis was performed to determine the strategic groups in each of the six identified subperiods. The results of this analysis are presented next.

5.2 IDENTIFICATION AND DESCRIPTION OF STRATEGIC GROUPS WITHIN EACH PERIOD

To identify the strategic groups within each SSTP, data on strategic variables was averaged for the duration of each SSTP, and then cluster analysis was performed on these means. Previous research has employed Ward's minimum variance method for clustering firms into strategic groups. But this method is biased towards generating equal sized clusters and is subject to the centroid drift problem (Punj and Stewart 1983). To overcome these problems, a two stage clustering program, where Ward's hierarchical agglomerative clustering is used in the first stage to generate seed values and the approximate number of clusters for iterative partitioning in the second stage, was employed.

Since hypothesis testing for stability and performance effects is totally dependent on correct identification of strategic groups, great care was exercised to accurately identify groups. Multiple methods were employed to arrive at the number of strategic groups/clusters. The first method employed was the cluster stopping rule recommended by Harrigan (1985) and Fiegenbaum and Thomas (1990), i.e.

- Clusters explain at least 65% of the overall variance in the data
- And, an additional cluster adds less than 5% to the variance explained

While the entire analysis in this study was carried out using the SPSS PC software program, this test was performed using the FastClus program in SAS, since the SPSS program output does not give the R^2 explained and the incremental change in R^2.

These results were corroborated by looking for breaks in the agglomeration schedule of hierarchical clustering routine and inspecting the scree plots (Everitt 1980). Then the procedure was reversed by running a discriminant analysis to verify the classification rates of the identified groups. To enhance the robustness of these results jackknifing procedures using a reduced set of variables and holdout sampling were employed. The results remained the same.

Finally, a MANOVA was run on identified clusters to see whether the clusters really differed on strategic scope and resource deployment commitments. Then an ANOVA was performed on every strategy variable, for each period, to establish on what competitive dimensions the identified strategic groups really differed. Tables 5.2 to 5.7, show the results of this analysis as well as the group mean and standard deviations on each strategic dimension. These group mean and standard deviations were employed to develop a profile of each cluster and to dynamically track these clusters over time. Figures 5.1 to 5.6 show the group membership of each firm within each SSTP. This is discussed next, along with an exposition of key changes between periods.

5.3 STRATEGIC GROUP DYNAMICS

In the first SSTP, four strategic groups are observed. (See table 5.2 and figure 5.1) A detailed description of each of these follows.

5.3.1 Strategic Groups in the Period 1974-79

GROUP 1: This is the *domestic retail banking* group, which primarily meet localized banking needs and are growing at the industry average growth rates, with their loan portfolio split almost evenly between real estate and commercial markets and deposit base tilted in favor of demand deposits. They are characterized by the lowest noninterest revenues, poor expense management and high capitalization. These banks largely depend on their deposit base for funding their asset growth and shy away from buying fed funds in the open market.

GROUP 2: The largest of all groups, this is the *global multirisk* cluster, which accounts for 63% of sample assets. This group has the highest degree of foreign exposure and is the largest purchaser of federal funds. It has the highest growth rate, noninterest revenues and fixed/time deposits, while having the lowest equity capital, real estate loans and noninterest expenses.

GROUP 3: The *diversified regionals*. This group is similar to the global group in its orientation, except that its deposit base is split evenly between demand and time deposits, and its foreign exposure is significantly less than the globals. Its growth rate is the lowest, but it is better capitalized than the global group, although its commercial and industrial loans and fed funds purchased are nearly at the same levels, while its real estate loans are higher than the global group.

GROUP 4: This is the *real estate oriented tier I regionals*. This group is below industry average in its fee based activities and purchase of federal funds. The focal point of its strategy is a concentration in real estate markets. It also has significantly less foreign exposure than the diversified regionals. The composition of its deposit base is not as spread out as the diversified group, although its participation in the commercial loan market is almost same as the diversified regional group. Its capitalization is better than both global and diversified regional group.

5.3.2 Key Changes in 1980-82 (See Table 5.3 and Figure 5.2)

Two new groups emerge. Group 2 is the aggressive acquirers group, which is characterized by high growth, highest capitalization, heavy involvement in wholesale markets, fee based activities, and a high degree of fed funds purchase. Group 5 is the trust banking group which is characterized by a focus on specialized trust and custodial business as indicated by an excessive contribution of noninterest revenues to its operations.

The domestic retail banking group diffuses across diversified regionals, the real estate oriented tier I regionals, and the newly formed aggressive acquirers group. The global group is highly stable with only Chemical Bank attempting a strategic repositioning and moving into the newly formed trust banking group. The diversified regional acquires thirteen new members, while losing nine firms. Four of these moved to the trust group and another four shifted to the aggressive acquirers group. The R.E oriented tier I regionals have one new entry, while losing nine firms: eight to the diversified regional and one to the trust banking group. This reflects a broadening of strategic focus by these firms. Provisions for loan-lease losses became a significant clustering dimension in this SSTP as opposed to the previous one.

5.3.3 Key Changes in 1983-85 (See Table 5.4 and Figure 5.3)

A new high growth retail oriented group composed of eight firms emerges. This group is distinct from the aggressive acquirers group in that it has targeted retail and conventional banking activities to fuel its growth, which is slower than aggressive acquirers group. It also funds its growth more by its deposit base as opposed to funding by fed funds by the aggressive acquirers group.

The diversified regional group has the maximum number of new entries - five from the aggressive acquirers group firms slowing down and four from trust banks retreating back to their original group, reflecting inability to execute the highly focused and specialized trust banking strategy. First Interstate and Fleet/Norstar moved into this group from real estate oriented tier I, reflecting their efforts to diversify their asset base. On the other hand, the global group is exactly same, although its share of aggregate sample assets goes down from 57% to 51%, reflecting increasing heterogeneity in the industry.

The aggressive acquirers group gained two new members (KeyCorp. and Suntrust) from the diversified regional group, while losing seven firms largely to the diversified regional group, reflecting slowing down by the firms. The remaining banks in the Aggressive acquirers group had a growth rate of nearly 100%. Finally, six banks moved into the specialized tier I group from the diversified regionals, indicating their failure to handle a diversified portfolio. Only one bank (Huntington) shifted from aggressive acquirers group to tier I group, reflecting a fundamental shift in its orientation from wholesale to retail, although it still had a growth rate of 66%.

5.3.4 Key Changes in 1986 (See Table 5.5 and Figure 5.4)

The industry exhibits maximum strategic heterogeneity in this time period. For the only time in the fifteen horizon of this study the global group splits up losing three members (Manufacturer's Hanover, Continental and Bank of America) to a new group composed of retracting globals withdrawing from foreign markets and refocusing on domestic retail markets, and weakening regionals with bad loans and poor capitalization. Chase Manhattan moves into the trust group and Bank of Boston retracts into the diversified regionals.

The aggressive acquirers group dissolves reflecting slowing down and imminent consolidation in the industry. The high growth retail oriented group remains largely stable, while picking up some members from the defunct Aggressive acquirers group. The trust group acquires six new members reflecting attempts by firms to duplicate this highly specialized and profitable strategy. Finally, while the regional groups are largely stable, a new group of troubled banks with a negative growth rate, high provisions, uncontrollable expenses, and below industry average capitalization emerges.

5.3.4 Key Changes in 1987 (See Table 5.6 and Figure 5.5)

This SSTP starts the first in the series of two dramatic change processes in a retracting, consolidating industry, thrown into chaos by exogenous shocks. Three groups dissolve. The high growth and Real estate oriented tier I groups merge to form a single group. The global group regains its three members lost to the transient retracting global+weakening regional group.

The troubled group undergoes a wholesale change, losing all its existing members and acquiring three new ones. The trust group again loses three members to diversified regional and the newly formed merged group. Finally, the diversified regionals is quite stable, except for absorbing five members from the dissolving global+weakening regional retracting group.

5.3.5 Key Changes in 1988   (See Table 5.7 and Figure 5.6)

The industry turns a full cycle after having gone through a tumultuous period. An increasing homogenization is visible, with three out of the four original groups from 1974-79 reappearing. State Street is the only survivor, albeit a very successful one, in the trust group. The rest of three groups are quite well defined with a high degree of strategic distance between cluster centroids, showing a crystallization of the industry structure.

There is an apparent diffusion of market power in the industry with the global group only accounting for 38% of the sample assets as opposed to 63% before deregulation.

5.4 RESULTS OF HYPOTHESIS TESTING

H1:   *During periods of severe environmental discontinuity, there will be significantly greater inter-group mobility.*

Table 5.8 shows the net changes in the number of strategic groups in each time period. An inspection of this table shows that the maximum number of changes occurred in 1980-82 and 1987 following the events which caused severe environmental shocks and discontinuity in the industry. These results support H1.

H2:   *Environmental discontinuities will be associated with the observance of negative risk return relationships at the firm level.*

For testing the relationship between risk and return, a least squares regression analysis was performed. The average return on assets for each time period was regressed on the standard deviation of ROAA for that period. Following Fiegenbaum & Thomas (1990), the standard deviation for single year SSTP's was computed by pooling them with the previous time period. ROAA was chosen as the representative performance indicator, because it is the most widely used industry performance measure.

Table 5.9 shows the R^2 values and beta weights of regression analysis[1]. As can be seen, a negative relationship exists between risk and return in the banking industry at all time periods. However, the strength of this relationship increases during the second and fifth SSTPs - the two periods of severe environmental discontinuity, thereby providing some indirect support for the hypothesized impact of environmental discontinuity in altering risk-return relationships. Also, a pattern of increasing association is observable between risk-return after the deregulation, reflecting the fiscal discipline which market mechanisms and price decontrols have brought to this industry.

H3A: *Performance difference measured in economic terms will exist between strategic groups during stable strategic time periods.*

A multivariate analysis of variance was performed to test for performance differences across strategic groups in each time period. Table 5.10 shows the results of this analysis. For 1987, PE ratios were excluded from the analysis since most banks made losses for that year, thereby rendering the price earnings multiples meaningless. Uniform support is found for this hypothesis at 99% confidence level in all time periods. However, the results of Univariate analysis on individual performance measures show that financial market measure - PE ratio is not significantly different across groups in four out of six time periods (see table 5.11).

H3B: *Within each period of stable strategic group structure, strategic groups will exhibit different levels of risk.*

Table 5.10 also shows the results of testing for risk exposure across strategic groups. Risk was measured as the temporal standard deviation of each performance measure within each time period. For the three single year time periods, risk was measured by computing the standard deviations on the pooled data from 1980 to the period in question. Thus, for 1986 the risk measures were based on six year data from 1980-86, while for 1988, they were based on eight years data from 1980-88. This procedure of pooling data for entire post-deregulation period rather than lagging one SSTP at time was thought to be more reliable because of the high degree of turbulence in this industry.

Significant risk differences were found across strategic groups at a .001 level of significance for three time periods and at .05 level of significance for two time periods. No statistically significant differences were observed for 1983-85 time period. However, the results of univariate testing showed that except for 1987, no risk differences are observed between strategic groups on individual performance measures (see table 5.11).

H3C: *Within each period of stable strategic group structure, strategic groups will exhibit dissimilar levels of risk-adjusted performance.*

Finally, the last facet of across group performance analysis involved testing for risk adjusted performance differences. As can be seen in table 5.10, MANOVA analysis showed that risk adjusted performance differences were present across strategic groups in the U.S. Banking industry only in 1988. These results were corroborated by univariate ANOVAs as shown in table 5.11.

H4: *Firms belonging to the same strategic group will not realize similar performance levels.*

To examine performance differences within groups unaggregated data on each bank was matched with its cluster membership within each time period. Then each of these clusters/strategic groups were individually examined for risk and performance differences. First, an analysis of risk differences was conducted using the Bartlett's variance homogeneity test. Table 5.12 shows the results of this analysis. An examination of this table shows that in 47 out of 85 tests no risk differences existed within the strategic groups. Further analysis shows that while in the period before deregulation, only 27% of tests pointed to the existence of similar risk levels within strategic groups, this number increased to 46.6% in 1980-82, 77.7% in 1983-85, and then fell again to 52.4% in 1986, shooting to 90% in 1987 (as before, risk measures on the PE were not meaningful in this time period because of sharp losses), and finally dropping back to 44.4% in 1988. The increase in the similarity of risk level between the members of the same strategic group in the periods following deregulation shows the increased effect of strategic groups in the industry after deregulation.

Then firm performance differences within each strategic group were examined using the analysis of variance. Since, the assumption of homogeneity of variance was violated for some groups, a nonparametric ANOVA - Kruskal Wallis was performed. Table 5.13 presents the results of this testing. The results for only the first three SSTPs are presented in this table. It is impossible to execute either parametric or nonparametric analysis of variance for single year time periods, because of limited data points. A visual inspection and an examination of the dispersion of performance values within strategic groups in the latter three SSTPs, indicated that the results are quite similar to the previous three time periods. In other words, strong support is found for the hypothesized within group performance differences.

H5:   *A model of intra industry performance difference that includes measures of firm capabilities together with strategic group membership as predictors will have more predictive validity (higher proportion of explained variance) than a model omitting capability measures.*

To test this hypothesis the 45 firms in the cross-sectional sample on which capability scores were available were assigned to group membership based on the results of 1988 industry map - the most recent time period in the longitudinal sample. One firm in the cross-sectional sample (Midlantic Bancorp.) did not appear in the longitudinal sample(it may be recalled that it was part of the original sample, but was dropped due to lack of data availability), and consequently was dropped, resulting in a final sample of 44 firms.

Forcing a reduced set of firms from the cross-sectional sample into 1988 clusters, may raise some questions about the validity of the procedure. However, a high degree of stability was observed among strategic group structures while performing cluster analysis on a reduced number of firms as discussed above. Hence, this procedure is deemed to be fairly reliable.

A regression analysis was performed to test for the contribution of group membership and organizational resources in explaining variance in organizational performance in both 1988 and 1990. The results are shown in tables 5.14A and 5.14B. Since organizational resources were highly correlated, they were factor analyzed into two factors - assets and skills for the purpose of this analysis. Assets consisted of efficiency, risk management, adequacy of the capital base, and asset quality, while skills were composed of technological expertise, innovation, and placing power. Management quality and depth, franchise and information asymmetries split evenly on the both the factors.

An examination of tables 5.14A and 5.14B, clearly shows that the addition of firm resources significantly adds to an explanation of intraindustry performance variation, thereby supporting hypothesis five. This relationship is more powerful in 1990 as opposed to 1988 in terms of the overall percentage of variation explained. They may result from the fact that 1988 was an unusual year for the industry. The industry was highly profitable in 1988 since banks had taken huge losses on their balance sheets the previous year to provide reserves for the LDC debt exposure. This "doctoring" of balance sheets coupled with a strong economy generated extraneous variance in the relationship between strategy, firm resource endowments, and performance.

The fact that cluster membership is almost nonsignificant while resource variables are highly significant in 1990 is interesting. It suggests the increasing importance of resources in shaping competition in the industry, as also the fact that strategic group membership in 1990 is not likely to be the same as in 1988.

H6:   *Firm resource bundles can be employed to identify meaningful strategic groups, as measured by the assessments of industry observers.*

To this exploratory hypothesis expert panel ratings on the ten resource variables were pooled and cluster analyzed using similar procedures as outlined in the longitudinal analysis. A five cluster solution was obtained, which looked very different form the clustering solutions obtained by using scope and resource deployment variables. Figure 5.7 shows the results of this analysis, while table 5.15 presents the group means, standard deviations, the results of MANOVA testing on cluster centroids, and the ANOVAs on individual clustering dimensions.

An inspection of table 5.15 shows that based on cluster centroids, group 2 is most well endowed group while group 5 is the least endowed. Their performance also follows a similar pattern, with group 2 being the "winners" and group 5 being the "losers". The rest of the three groups fall between these two extreme groups with group 1 being closer to group five, while groups three and four are more proximate to group two.

It is interesting to observe that while all groups have strong franchises (above industry average), they don't have uniform capabilities to exploit those franchises. Again, although group 4 has the highest placing power and a strong technological expertise (its coefficient of variation (mean/standard deviation) is 7.60 vs. 7.15 for group2) and innovation capability (c.v. of 10.08 vs. 7.29 for group2), it is not able to exploit/convert them into a significant competitive advantage. Perhaps its weak risk management capability coupled with its relative inefficiency and a moderate capital base prevent it from fully deploying its capabilities in other areas.

Group 3 outperforms Group 4, but a comparison of the two reveals that they are quite similar in their resource configurations, with Group 4 scoring higher on some and group 3 on others. The key difference is between their risk management capability and asset quality. Indeed, risk management seems to be a core skill in this industry. While, I continue this analysis of the resource based strategic groups in the next chapter, a preliminary examination appears to show that some resources confer a disproportionate degree of competitive advantage in the banking industry, while some others seem to work only in combination with other resources.

The meaningfulness of these groupings is hard to determine, given that they represent a fundamentally different way of conceptualizing industry competitive dynamics. However, the implications of this framework for strategic management are quite significant and is discussed in the next chapter. Members of the expert panel found them to be very interesting and instructive. Their acceptance was certainly facilitated by the fact industry analysts increasingly view the industry competition as being denominated in terms of organizational skills (WSJ, Mar. 23,1991). The best and perhaps the sole quantitative or statistical method of determining the validity of these groupings is look at the percentage of differential performance across groups explained. This issue is investigated by hypothesis seven below.

H7:   *Increased differential performance effects will be associated with resource based strategic groups, as compared to product market based groups.*

To compare the percentage of performance variation across groups explained by the resource based groups with conventional product market strategy based groups, ANOVA tests were performed across strategic groups in all time periods to compute the R^2 figures for each performance dimension in each time period. Table 5.16 presents the results of this analysis. As can be seen uniform support is found for this hypothesis across all three performance dimensions.

5.5 LIMITATIONS

The findings of this study should be evaluated in the light of the following limitations: First, the non-inclusion of foreign banks, who constitute a significant competitive force particularly in the wholesale banking markets, is a clear limitation. These banks could not be included due to non-availability of data. It is not known whether they would form a different strategic group or belong to existing strategic groups, thereby inhibiting a fuller understanding of the strategic group phenomenon.

Second, the measures of market based performance and risk are relatively weak. Future research should employ the Capital Asset Pricing Model to get cumulative abnormal returns and betas - the market based assessment of performance. There is currently a debate going on between some scholars who question the whole mean variance approach to measuring risk (See Ruefli, 1990; Bromiley, 1991; and Ruefli, 1991). It may be more appropriate to use the variation in analysts earning forecast available on the IBES database as a measure of risk. This measure could not be employed in this study since IBES does not report data as far back as 1974.

Third, while the scope and resource deployment variable specification was quite rigorous, a further improvement in this process is possible in order to capture finer points of banking strategy. For example, the real estate portfolio might have been decomposed into commercial and residential components. Similarly, measures of contingent commitments and letters of credit outstanding might have captured "off balance sheet" activity - a significant dimension of competition in the banking industry. Again, data limitations precluded the use of these variables.

Fourth, while the overlying of a cross-sectional research design on a longitudinal research design is relatively novel, it should be recognized that the findings of this endeavor should be treated as purely exploratory. This is so, because there is a limited comparability between two samples in terms of membership and time period.

Finally, this study is subject to the problem of generalizability inherent in all single industry studies. The relative correspondence of the results with findings from previous single industry studies (especially Fiegenbaum's (1987) insurance industry study) inspires some confidence, however. This leads one to speculate that similar phenomenon may be observed in other financial services industries, in particular, and service industries in general.

Table 5.1 Identification of SSTP's

Period	# Years	F value	Significant Industry Events
1974-76	6	1.43 (.009)	
1980-82	3	1.89 (.000)	Passage of Depository Institutions Deregulation and Monetary Control Act
1983-85	3	1.53 (.007)	Passage of Garn St. Germain Act 1982
1986	1	1.92 (.000)	Lagged effect of Mexican Debt Rescheduling
1987	1	3.65 (.000)	LDC debt crises
1988	1	2.11 (.000)	Unusually healthy year for the recuperatîng industry

Notes: 1.) F values for the Box's M test.
2.) The values in the parentheses indicate the significance level.

Table 5.2 Strategic Groups in the Period 1974-1979: MANOVA and ANOVA
Test results, Group centroids and Standard deviations (in parentheses)

Strategy Variable	MANOVA F(WILKS) = 14.424 (P=0.000)				F(ANOVA)
	SGI (N=13)	SGII (n=11)	SGIII (n=20)	SGIV (n=24)	
RE	15.85 (3.28)	4.87 (2.45)	10.0 (2.98)	19.68 (6.69)	45.6(0.000)
CI	18.19 (3.93)	16.89 (3.84)	19.21 (4.65)	19.16 (3.82)	1.1(0.370)
DEM	42.44 (3.08)	26.76 (7.67)	42.71 (5.87)	33.48 (8.20)	25.5(0.000)
TIM	31.72 (7.18)	69.59 (8.03)	44.66 (6.03)	44.35 (6.54)	64.4(0.000)
FOREXP	0.63 (1.09)	33.44 (6.43)	9.62 (6.20)	2.78 (2.73)	133.0(0.000)
NIR	12.47 (2.71)	23.50 (5.10)	21.06 (3.69)	12.50 (3.90)	34.1(0.000)
LEV	1.24 (0.45)	0.64 (0.21)	0.85 (0.35)	0.99 (0.76)	2.7(0.053)
NPF	5.24 (2.18)	7.20 (3.68)	10.71 (3.49)	6.59 (2.84)	10.0(0.000)
GROWTH	10.11 (2.62)	14.52 (6.13)	8.85 (4.12)	9.09 (3.30)	5.54(0.002)
CS	26.44 (2.50)	15.58 (2.43)	21.07 (4.43)	21.37 (3.53)	19.12(0.000)
PROV	0.36 (0.10)	0.36 (0.11)	0.32 (0.17)	0.33 (0.16)	0.35(0.793)

Table 5.3 Strategic Groups in the Period 1980-82: MANOVA and ANOVA Test results, Group centroids and Standard deviations (in parentheses)

Strategy Variable	MANOVA F(WILKS) = 9.625 (P=0.00)					
	SGI (n=10)	SGII (n=15)	SGIII (n=22)	SGIV (n=14)	SGV (n=7)	F(ANOVA)
RE	5.89 (3.95)	12.39 (3.39)	14.66 (4.31)	21.38 (5.30)	10.84 (4.19)	19.79(0.000)
CI	16.92 (5.65)	24.19 (4.73)	20.67 (3.87)	24.47 (5.76)	20.75 (5.71)	2.82(0.032)
DEM	17.84 (5.38)	25.46 (3.50)	35.95 (6.64)	24.57 (3.90)	27.93 (3.48)	29.25(0.000)
TIM	79.82 (5.98)	55.76 (4.50)	43.30 (6.59)	51.85 (3.35)	57.80 (5.94)	84.64(0.000)
FOREXP	36.77 (3.44)	8.31 (4.75)	2.93 (3.64)	3.52 (3.82)	20.90 (5.71)	129.4(0.000)
NIR	26.70 (6.91)	23.59 (5.64)	18.73 (8.22)	15.84 (3.17)	27.94 (3.99)	9.50(0.000)
LEV	0.46 (0.17)	0.91 (0.77)	0.72 (0.38)	0.85 (0.56)	0.58 (0.35)	1.62(0.181)
NPF	8.79 (3.73)	12.29 (4.56)	11.88 (4.02)	7.92 (2.67)	12.63 (2.88)	3.93(0.007)
GROWTH	10.15 (6.86)	17.99 (7.08)	10.79 (6.27)	9.01 (4.61)	10.50 (3.36)	4.80(0.002)
CS	9.94 (1.69)	13.91 (2.21)	17.85 (2.62)	15.85 (1.87)	12.45 (3.03)	22.62(0.000)
PROV	0.31 (0.10)	0.28 (0.10)	0.29 (0.10)	0.43 (0.19)	0.25 (0.03)	4.16(0.005)

Table 5.4 Strategic Groups in the Period 1983-85: MANOVA and ANOVA Test results, Group centroids and Standard deviations (in parentheses)

Strategy Variable	MANOVA F(WILKS) = 8.829 (P=0.000)						F(ANOVA)
	SGI (n=10)	SGII (n=11)	SGIII (n=7)	SGIV (n=20)	SGV (n=17)	SGVI (n=3)	
RE	7.11 (4.94)	12.37 (3.67)	17.74 (3.71)	13.27 (3.68)	19.66 (6.00)	6.13 (2.53)	9.62(0.000)
CI	17.90 (8.49)	25.78 (4.57)	21.25 (3.73)	25.75 (5.10)	26.01 (6.28)	17.63 (4.37)	4.17(0.002)
DEM	17.46 (5.24)	23.11 (2.77)	30.74 (6.81)	24.94 (6.30)	23.37 (5.03)	37.04 (12.49)	7.43(0.000)
TIM	79.49 (5.84)	55.95 (9.26)	37.67 (7.83)	60.15 (8.15)	44.86 (5.36)	46.74 (1.52)	42.38(0.000)
FOREXP	34.14 (4.75)	4.79 (3.96)	2.38 (2.60)	9.97 (7.50)	1.92 (2.52)	6.78 (6.17)	58.08(0.000)
NIR	25.49 (9.50)	20.48 (4.20)	16.88 (3.54)	22.63 (4.75)	16.58 (4.65)	37.65 (5.38)	8.87(0.000)
LEV	0.44 (0.18)	0.82 (0.52)	0.90 (0.38)	0.58 (0.38)	0.81 (0.43)	0.86 (0.48)	2.12(0.074)
NPF	8.17 (4.10)	13.72 (6.15)	9.27 (3.10)	11.45 (3.87)	8.65 (3.55)	15.42 (4.45)	3.09(0.015)
GROWTH	6.41 (7.92	33.81 (7.92)	29.50 (9.52)	11.69 (3.11)	10.47 (4.15)	11.84 (6.33)	26.62(0.000) (7.15)
CS	15.07 (3.72)	18.58 (2.17)	20.94 (2.10)	18.47 (2.64)	20.81 (2.33)	19.93 (1.90)	7.30(0.000)
PROV	0.59 (0.37)	0.37 (0.11)	0.29 (0.11)	0.45 (0.19)	0.57 (0.22)	0.38 (0.30)	2.69(0.029)

Table 5.5 Strategic Groups in the Period 1986: MANOVA and ANOVA Test results, Group centroids, and Standard deviations (in parentheses)

MANOVA F(WILKS) = 10.114 (P=0.000)

Strategy Variable	SGI (n=8)	SGII (n=18)	SGIII (n=10)	SGIV (n=9)	SGV (n=5)	SGVI (n=13)	SGVII (n=5)	F(ANOVA)
RE	11.97 (5.19)	16.40 (4.62)	24.82 (9.21)	10.15 (4.20)	7.35 (6.84)	13.67 (3.17)	22.95 (3.16)	9.34(0.000)
CI	26.95 (5.11)	27.91 (5.61)	25.76 (6.25)	18.91 (5.49)	11.89 (5.93)	28.19 (4.59)	25.94 (6.00)	5.96(0.000)
DEM	22.50 (4.26)	24.31 (4.76)	24.51 (6.41)	32.47 (13.58)	17.67 (6.93)	27.48 (4.83)	23.99 (4.48)	3.52(0.005)
TIM	77.50 (4.26)	38.64 (4.42)	35.43 (5.37)	42.38 (6.37)	77.96 (7.45)	72.52 (4.83)	45.07 (9.23)	67.2(0.000)
FOREXP	14.08 (10.9)	1.83 (1.99)	2.35 (3.14)	14.02 (11.6)	32.98 (3.25)	4.74 (5.16)	1.62 (1.59)	19.1(0.000)
NIR	22.13 (2.94)	15.80 (3.05)	15.97 (3.77)	30.20 (10.2)	35.78 (6.84)	19.60 (3.19)	20.87 (2.41)	19.3(0.000)
LEV	0.39 (0.34)	1.36 (0.78)	0.78 (0.55)	0.80 (0.34)	0.67 (0.39)	0.76 (0.55)	0.62 (0.38)	2.05(0.072)
NPF	10.73 (7.29)	9.97 (4.93)	9.37 (6.25)	9.90 (4.58)	9.64 (5.89)	11.57 (4.96)	9.94 (1.92)	0.22(0.969)
GROWTH	2.94 (7.67)	16.00 (7.12)	52.52 (12.3)	11.82 (5.29)	9.75 (5.34)	24.67 (9.04)	-5.00 (7.85)	37.7(0.000)
CS	26.43 (5.24)	24.91 (2.25)	25.16 (2.18)	24.79 (3.57)	19.00 (6.16)	24.79 (4.30)	36.46 (6.40)	9.46(0.000)
PROV	0.97 (0.61)	0.51 (0.21)	0.49 (0.22)	0.54 (0.28)	0.66 (0.39)	0.57 (0.26)	1.95 (0.99)	10.5(0.000)

Table 5.6 Strategic Groups in the Period 1987: MANOVA and ANOVA Test results, Group centroids, and Standard deviations (in parentheses)

| Strategy Variable | MANOVA F(WILKS) = 12.649 (P=0.000) | | | | | F(ANOVA) |
	SGI (n=19)	SGII (n=32)	SGIII (n=3)	SGIV (n=6)	SGV (n=8)	
RE	14.43 (4.69)	22.64 (8.56)	18.93 (6.27)	12.19 (4.90)	8.87 (6.46)	5.5(0.000)
CI	27.19 (5.24)	25.12 (6.14)	27.67 (2.96)	18.70 (5.18)	15.92 (9.18)	5.6(0.000)
DEM	22.24 (4.14)	20.86 (4.36)	23.35 (6.11)	29.12 (14.45)	16.44 (5.56)	3.6(0.007)
TIM	77.76 (4.14)	43.46 (6.49)	69.45 (10.21)	46.83 (7.18)	80.47 (4.85)	102.4(0.000)
FOREXP	4.64 (4.92)	2.34 (2.30)	4.98 (3.73)	19.20 (10.18)	31.62 (5.54)	53.3(0.000)
NIR	20.15 (3.79)	16.36 (3.83)	22.31 (6.46)	32.76 (11.70)	33.34 (6.91)	18.6(0.000)
LEV	0.72 (0.52)	1.00 (0.80)	0.41 (0.51)	0.84 (0.39)	0.57 (0.37)	1.0(0.417)
NPF	10.70 (4.78)	10.09 (3.81)	10.88 (4.39)	9.98 (5.59)	7.19 (5.26)	70.6(0.000)
GROWTH	10.04 (11.76)	25.07 (34.09)	-12.58 (5.09)	9.66 (11.54)	3.84 (11.84)	2.3(0.058)
CS	26.57 (3.49)	29.58 (5.19)	49.68 (10.24)	33.00 (3.86)	31.52 (7.94)	10.7(0.000)
PROV	0.81 (0.48)	1.01 (0.64)	3.91 (1.90)	1.56 (0.77)	2.00 (0.84)	13.0(0.000)

Table 5.7 Strategic Groups in the Period 1988: MANOVA and ANOVA Test results, Group centroids, and Standard deviations (in parentheses)

Strategy Variable	MANOVA F(WILKS) = 32.078 (P=0.000)				
	SGI (n=19)	SGII (n=38)	SGIII (n=10)	SGIV (n=1)	F(ANOVA)
RE	17.32 (4.63)	21.68 (9.34)	11.53 (7.83)	2.68 (0.00)	4.85(0.004)
CI	28.41 (5.89)	25.10 (6.26)	15.35 (8.71)	15.61 (0.00)	9.02(0.000)
DEM	21.67 (4.49)	20.41 (4.38)	17.20 (5.83)	51.51 (4.84)	19.4(0.000)
TIM	78.33 (4.49)	46.63 (7.15)	75.06 (12.26)	48.49 (0.000)	86.7(0.000)
FOREXP	4.86 (4.44)	2.67 (3.08)	28.69 (5.21)	13.49 (0.00)	120.2(0.000)
NIR	19.82 (4.20)	18.33 (6.56)	33.10 (7.21)	55.09 (0.00)	27.0(0.000)
LEV	0.59 (0.52)	0.93 (0.93)	0.47 (0.47)	0.44 (0.00)	1.80(0.156)
NPF	8.60 (4.00)	9.84 (4.49)	7.03 (5.42)	21.09 (0.00)	3.78(0.015)
GROWTH	8.56 (8.76)	9.33 (10.5)	1.46 (6.12)	20.37 (0.00)	1.70(0.175)
CS	23.93 (5.41)	24.64 (3.63)	18.51 (5.26)	27.58 (0.00)	6.49(0.001)
PROV	0.48 (0.27)	0.55 (0.23)	0.40 (0.30)	0.22 (0.00)	1.51(0.219)

Table 5.8 Net changes in strategic groups

	1974-79	1980-82	SSTP 1983-85	1986	1987	1988
No. of strategic groups	4	5	6	7	5	4
New strategic groups	-	2	1	2	1	0
Strategic groups dissolved	-	1	0	1	3	1
Total change index	-	3	1	3	4	1

Table 5.9 Firm level risk-return regression analysis

Time Period	R^2	F-statistic	Beta	T-value
1974-79	0.186	15.054[*]	-0.431	-3.880[*]
1980-82	0.284	26.116[*]	-0.532	-5.110[*]
1983-85	0.518	70.923[*]	-0.720	-8.422[*]
1986	0.467	57.768[*]	-0.683	-7.601[*]
1987	0.951	1269.1[*]	-0.975	-35.63[*]
1988	0.080	5.622[**]	-0.282	-2.371[**]

* $p<.001$; ** $p<.05$.

Table 5.10 Strategic groups and performance differences:
MANOVA results for each performance dimension

Performance Dimension	Stable Strategic Time Period					
	I 1974-79	II 1980-82	III 1983-85	IV 1986	V 1987	VI 1988
Economic	7.84^{***}	6.40^{***}	3.52^{***}	6.35^{***}	7.76^{***}	6.18^{***}
Risk	3.43^{***}	1.92^{*}	1.60	1.87^{*}	13.7^{***}	3.83^{***}
Risk Adjusted	1.40	0.85	0.98	0.82	1.13	2.64^{**}

Notes:
1. F(Wilks) values and their significance levels are shown
   in the table.
   *** $p < .001$; ** $p < .01$; * $p < .05$.

2. The analysis for 1987 does not include PE ratios.

Table 5.11 Strategic groups and performance differences: ANOVA results for individual performance measures

Period	ROAA	PE	PPE
	Economic Performance Levels		
1974-79	2.81 (0.046)	0.82 (0.487)	5.72 (0.002)
1980-82	3.99 (0.006)	1.98 (0.109)	6.54 (0.000)
1983-85	3.87 (0.004)	0.86 (0.511)	0.70 (0.625)
1986	4.59 (0.001)	0.60 (0.731)	11.6 (0.000)
1987	17.2 (0.000)	- - -	15.9 (0.000)
1988	0.44 (0.724)	13.6 (0.000)	0.59 (0.625)
	Risk Exposure		
1974-79	2.47 (0.070)	0.78 (0.509)	3.94 (0.012)
1980-82	1.72 (0.157)	1.60 (0.186)	1.57 (0.193)
1983-85	1.37 (0.249)	0.66 (0.653)	1.91 (0.107)
1986	1.70 (0.137)	0.49 (0.812)	1.44 (0.215)
1987	15.7 (0.000)	- - -	16.1 (0.000)
1988	0.59 (0.627)	0.55 (0.652)	4.66 (0.005)
	Risk-Adjusted Performance		
1974-79	1.12 (0.349)	1.60 (0.197)	0.44 (0.728)
1980-82	0.96 (0.599)	0.79 (0.537)	0.89 (0.477)
1983-85	0.44 (0.816)	1.86 (0.114)	0.73 (0.606)
1986	0.72 (0.791)	0.37 (0.896)	1.07 (0.392)
1987	0.53 (0.471)	- - -	1.53 (0.224)
1988	2.99 (0.037)	5.68 (0.002)	3.28 (0.027)

Notes:
1. F values and their significance levels (in parentheses) are shown in the table.

2. The analysis for the year 1987 does not include the PE ratios.

Table 5.12 Analysis of within group performance differences on individual performance measures (Kruskall-Wallace one-way ANOVA)

SSTP	Strategic Group	X^2 (Significance of X^2)		
		ROAA	PE	PPE
1974-79	SG1	48.1(.000)	36.5(.000)	42.7(.000)
	SG2	54.4(.000)	33.5(.000)	55.4(.000)
	SG3	80.2(.000)	34.6(.000)	94.6(.000)
	SG4	110.6(.000)	62.0(.000)	107.4(.000)
1980-82	SG1	22.8(.007)	19.8(.019)	21.7(.010)
	SG2	34.1(.002)	31.6(.005)	39.5(.000)
	SG3	38.5(.011)	48.3(.000)	42.8(.003)
	SG4	35.9(.000)	16.8(.207)	35.4(.000)
	SG5	16.4(.012)	16.3(.012)	17.2(.009)
1983-85	SG1	27.1(.001)	20.2(.017)	23.9(.005)
	SG2	23.9(.004)	12.1(.207)	23.6(.005)
	SG3	20.1(.005)	10.9(.142)	16.5(.021)
	SG4	44.8(.000)	22.3(.173)	46.0(.000)
	SG5	43.4(.001)	30.1(.036)	40.5(.002)
	SG6	7.20(.027)	6.49(.039)	5.96(.051)

Table 5.13   Comparison of risk differences between members of the
same strategic group (Bartlett-Box'M F-test)

Period	Strategic Group	SROAA	F-value (significance of F) SPE	SPPE
1974-79	SG1	3.4(.003)	2.7(.012)	1.5(.159)
	SG2	3.2(.000)	1.4(.173)	2.3(.009)
	SG3	1.6(.042)	10.4(.000)	1.1(.342)
	SG4	3.1(.000)	2.2(.001)	1.5(.049)
1980-82	SG1	1.7(.095)	2.8(.003)	2.4(.012)
	SG2	1.3(.184)	2.4(.002)	1.1(.339)
	SG3	3.2(.000)	3.6(.000)	2.3(.001)
	SG4	2.0(.019)	8.2(.000)	1.2(.258)
	SG5	0.9(.488)	0.8(.560)	5.5(.770)
1983-85	SG1	1.8(.072)	3.6(.000)	2.5(.008)
	SG2	1.2(.301)	0.1(1.00)	0.9(.489)
	SG3	0.5(.817)	1.4(.201)	0.5(.864)
	SG4	1.2(.301)	1.6(.071)	1.3(.185)
	SG5	2.2(.003)	2.4(.002)	1.5(.102)
	SG6	1.2(.293)	1.4(.249)	0.3(.769)
1986	SG1	1.1(.354)	4.5(.000)	1.3(.269)
	SG2	2.5(.001)	2.9(.000)	0.8(.691)
	SG3	1.4(.198)	0.6(.809)	0.7(.698)
	SG4	2.8(.005)	2.1(.039)	0.9(.504)
	SG5	3.2(.014)	3.6(.007)	2.9(.021)
	SG6	2.1(.014)	1.3(.190)	1.7(.057)
	SG7	1.6(.171)	8.5(.000)	0.9(.447)
1987	SG1	1.4(.150)	-	1.5(.116)
	SG2	1.6(.033)	-	0.9(.551)
	SG3	0.5(.593)	-	0.6(.569)
	SG4	1.0(.453)	-	1.1(.349)
	SG5	0.4(.918)	-	0.4(.901)
1988	SG1	2.1(.008)	7.7(.000)	1.6(.054)
	SG2	1.6(.028)	2.6(.000)	0.9(.665)
	SG3	0.4(.910)	3.1(.007)	0.9(.510)

Table 5.14   Regression analysis of cluster membership and firm resources on performance variables.

A) Regression analysis of cluster membership and firm resources on 1988 performance variables.

Performance Variable	Overall R^2	F(value)	Incremental Contribution of Assets & Skills to R^2	Significance (F-value)
ROAA	.162	2.782**	.080	2.152*
PPE	.350	7.187***	.091	2.908**
PE	.138	2.238*	.132	3.069**

* $p<.10$; ** $p<.05$; *** $p<.001$

B) Regression analysis of cluster membership and firm resources on 1990 performance variables.

Performance Variable	Overall R^2	F(value)	Incremental Contribution of Assets & Skills to R^2	Significance (F-value)
ROAA	.643	13.700***	.599	31.94***
PPE	.644	24.18***	.589	33.12***
PE	.280	5.197**	.260	7.239**

** $p<.01$; *** $p<.001$

Table 5.15: Resource based strategic groups: MANOVA and ANOVA test results; cluster centroids and standard deviations

| Resource Variable | MANOVA; F(Wilks)= 6.17 (p=.000) | | | | | |
	SGI (n=13)	SGII (n=13)	SGIII (n=7)	SGIV (n=7)	SGV (n=5)	F(ANOVA)
MQD	3.91 (.323)	5.92 (.615)	5.20 (.624)	4.86 (.468)	4.72 (.430)	46.4(.000)
FRAN	4.44 (.538)	5.81 (.444)	5.32 (.550)	5.20 (.773)	4.71 (.607)	10.4(.000)
AQ	3.34 (.488)	5.84 (.759)	4.83 (.486)	3.48 (.600)	2.04 (.402)	52.9(.000)
TE	3.85 (.477)	5.56 (.778)	4.32 (.468)	5.12 (.674)	3.28 (.311)	20.9(.000)
PP	4.08 (.727)	4.99 (.836)	4.16 (.167)	5.00 (.408)	3.19 (.572)	9.36(.000)
CAPB	3.81 (.575)	6.08 (.673)	4.75 (.588)	4.12 (1.01)	2.31 (.775)	32.1(.000)
EFF	3.96 (.515)	5.67 (.526)	5.16 (.325)	4.36 (.866)	3.55 (1.10)	17.1(.000)
INOV	3.84 (.402)	5.50 (.754)	4.22 (.279)	5.06 (.502)	3.26 (.611)	23.8(.000)
RM	3.71 (.433)	5.99 (.552)	5.16 (.317)	3.90 (.456)	2.13 (.533)	79.5(.000)
IA	4.02 (.220)	5.61 (.421)	4.47 (.293)	4.57 (.485)	3.32 (.238)	53.3(.000)

AVERAGE

MQD	FRAN	AQ	TE	PP	CAPB	EFF	INOV	RM	IA
4.72	5.12	4.17	4.55	4.40	4.49	4.66	4.50	4.45	4.56
(1.14)	(.768)	(1.42)	(1.01)	(.870)	(1.38)	(1.01)	(.969)	(1.35)	(.835)

Table 5.16 ANOVA - R^2 fit for individual performance measures

SSTP	ROA	F-value	PE	F-value	PPE	F-value
1974-79	.116	2.812 (.046)	.037	0.821 (.487)	.212	5.724 (.002)
1980-82	.202	3.993 (.006)	.112	1.977 (.109)	.293	6.540 (.000)
1983-85	.238	3.869 (.004)	.064	0.863 (.511)	.053	0.701 (.625)
1986	.320	4.890 (.000)	.051	0.538 (.778)	.444	7.999 (.000)
1987	.386	5.786 (.000)	----	----	.367	6.162 (.000)
1988	.021	0.442 (.724)	.028	0.588 (.625)	.402	13.68 (.000)
Resource based groups	.594	14.27 (.000)	.336	4.928 (.003)	.509	10.09 (.000)

Notes: 1.) Numbers in parentheses are the significance
levels of F-Values.
2.) PE values for 1987 are not meaningful.

Figure 5.1: Strategic Group Map Of The U.S. Banking Industry (1974 - 1979)

Domestic Retail Bank	Assets ($ MM)	Global Multirisk Bank	Assets ($ MM)	Diversified Regionals Bank	Assets ($ MM)	Tier I RE Oriented Regionals Bank	Assets ($ MM)
Banponce Corp.	1591	Republic NY	2490	Bk. of New England	1719	Old Kent	1346
KeyCorp.	1751	Bk. of Boston	10241	Riggs Natl.	2029	First Maryland	1545
United Bks. of CO	1715	First Chicago	22474	INB Finl.	2040	Marshall & Ilsley	1583
Banc One	1902	Bankers Trust	23923	State Street	2071	Dominion	1608
Huntington	1910	Continental	25775	First TN Natl.	2102	First Empire	1653
Commerce Bancshares	1997	Chemical	29235	Shawmut	2276	Signet	1898
Suntrust	2073	J.P. Morgan	32375	First Union	2456	Society Corp.	2129
AmSouth	2099	Manny Hanny	34933	Mercantile	3380	C&S Sovran	2160
Midlantic	2135	Chase Manhattan	51441	Natl. City	3505	UJB Finl.	2164
Baybanks	2318	CitiCorp.	75107	PNC Finl.	3837	Equimark	2420
First Fidelity	2576	Bk. of America	81055	Wachovia	4001	Fleet/Norstar	2494
Barnett	2757			Firstar	4219	First Security Utah	2625
Crestar Finl.	2815			Northern Trust	4294	MNC Finl.	2827
				NCNB	4729	Manufacturers Natl.	3527
				Corestates	4849	US BanCorp.	3604
				Bk. of NY	6104	Southeast	3776
				First City Texas	6208	Valley Natl.	3843
				NBD Bancorp.	8292	Comerica	3895
				Mellon	10567	Michigan Natl.	4141
				Security Pacific	18676	Ameritrust	4555
						First Bk. Sys.	9001
						Norwest	9275
						Wells Fargo	15428
						First Interstate	22541
AGGREGATE	**27639**		**389049**		**97354**		**110038**

Figure 5.2: Strategic Group Map Of The U.S. Banking Industry (1980 - 1982)

Global Multilatik Bank	Assets ($ MM)	Agresive Acquirers Bank	Diversified Regionals Bank	Assets ($ MM)	Tier I RE Oriented Regs. Bank	Assets ($ MM)	Trust Banking Assets ($ MM)	Trust Banking Bank	Assets ($ MM)
Republic NY	7811	Old Kent	INB Finl.	2180	First Empire	2546	1898	Riggs Natl.	3511
Bk. of Boston	17008	Signet	KeyCorp.	2862	Dominion	2607	2827	Northern Trust	6113
First Chicago	32713	First Maryland	Marshall & Ils.	2908	Equimark	2649	3025	Southeast	6527
Bankers Trust	36281	Huntington	Banponce Corp.	3757	C&S Sovran	2682	3264	Bk. of NY	11536
Continental	43987	Society Corp.	UJB Finl.	3792	Fleet/Norstar	2891	4070	NBD BanCorp.	11807
J.P. Morgan	54703	Banc One	AmSouth	3831	Crestar Finl.	2973	4076	Mellon	18300
Manny Hanny	59557	Bk. of NE	Commerce Banc	4133	First Sec. UT	3024	4124	Chemical	44845
Chase	78297	First Union	First TN Natl.	4916	Manf. Natl.	3152	5093		
Bk. of America	118332	Natl. City	United Bks. CO	5901	US BanCorp.	3186	5430		
CitiCorp.	121383	Comerica	Shawmut	6400	Ameritrust	3236	5628		
		PNC Finl.	State Street	6927	Michigan Natl.	3437	6163		
		First City TX	Baybanks	8820	Norwest	3460	15707		
		First Bk. Sys.	Midlantic	14044	Wells Fargo	3940	23890		
		Security Pacific	Suntrust	15095	First Interstate	4009	36659		
			First Fidelity	32595		4297			
			MNC Finl.			4540			
			Firstar			4695			
			Mercantile			5158			
			Barnett			5622			
			Corestates			6269			
			Wachovia			6279			
			Valley Natl.			6351			
AGGREGATE	570072			118161		87003	121854		102639

STRATEGIC GROUP MAP OF THE U.S. BANKING INDUSTRY (1983 - 1985)

GROUP 1 ASSETS ($MM)	GROUP 1 BANK	GROUP 2 ASSETS ($MM)	GROUP 2 BANK	GROUP 3 ASSETS BANK ($MM)	GROUP 4 ASSETS ($MM)	GROUP 4 BANK	GROUP 5 ASSETS ($MM)	GROUP 5 BANKS	GROUP 6 ASSETS ($MM)	GROUP 6 BANK	ASSETS ($MM)
12608	Republic NY	4018	Old Kent	Baybanks	5363	INB Finl.	3606	First Empire	2287	Banponce Corp.	3548
23305	Bk. of Boston	5243	Signet	Shawmut	6403	Marshall & Ils.	4020	Equimark	2700	State Street	5147
34346	Continental	2411	KeyCorp.	Midlantic	7982	UJB Finl.	4038	Dominion	4277	Northern Trust	7055
38354	First Chicago	6289	C&S Sovran	C&S Sovran	8382	First Maryland	4085	United Bks. CO	4311		
45264	Bankers Trust	9067	Banc One	First Fidelity	9906	Riggs Natl.	5107	Commerce Banc	4339		
63841	J.P. Morgan	10120	Bk. of NE	Natl. City	10488	Firstar	5685	AmSouth	4382		
72191	Manny Hanny	10230	First Union	Wachovia	11425	Fleet/Norstar	6202	First TN Natl.	4841		
85497	Chase	12570	Suntrust	Barnett	12242	Manf. Natl.	6335	First Sec. UT	5115		
119132	Bk. of America	15297	PNC Finl.			Comerica	9319	Huntington	5747		
152946	CitiCorp.	16080	NCNB			Corestates	9839	Mercantile	6072		
						NBD BancCorp.	14718	Center Finl.	6485		
						Bk. of NY	15480	Ameritrust	6810		
						First City TX	17134	MNC Finl.	6939		
						First Bk. Sys.	22931	Michigan Natl.	6957		
						Mellon	30147	US BancCorp.	7452		
						First Interstate	46319	Valley Natl.	8951		
						Security Pacific	46668	Southeast	9935		
						Chemical	53464	Norwest	20853		
								Wells Fargo	28210		
AGGREGATE 647484		91325			72191		305097		146663		15750

Figure 5.4

STRATEGIC GROUP MAP OF THE U.S. BANKING INDUSTRY (1986)

GROUP 1 ASSETS ($MM)	GROUP 1 BANK	GROUP 2 BANK	GROUP 3 ASSETS ($MM)	GROUP 3 BANK	GROUP 4 ASSETS ($MM)	GROUP 4 BANK	GROUP 5 ASSETS ($MM)	GROUP 5 BANKS	GROUP 6 ASSETS ($MM)	GROUP 6 BANK	GROUP 7 ASSETS ($MM)	GROUP 7 BANK	ASSETS ($MM)
9061	Society Corp.	Equimark	2481	UJB Finl.	8024	Banponce	4532	Republic NY	17665	INB Finl.	5106	United Bk. CO	4837
9983	Comerica	First Empire	2919	Ameritrust	11068	First TN Natl.	5556	First Chicago	39148	First Maryland	5487	First Sec. UT	5080
20709	Bk. of NY	Commerce Banc	5293	Fleet/Norstar	11690	Riggs Natl.	6253	Bankers Trust	56420	Old Kent	5582	Mercantile	6586
28012	First Bk. Sys.	Dominion	5921	Shawmut	13879	Firstar	7090	J.P. Morgan	76039	Marshall & Ils.	6001	First City TX	13861
32809	Continental	AmSouth	5943	C&S Sovran	14952	State Street	7190	CitiCorp	196124	Manf. Natl.	8110	Norwest	21559
34499	Mellon	Baybanks	7628	Midlantic	17185	Northern Trust	9090			KeyCorp.	9073		
74397	Manny Hanny	Michigan Natl.	7672	Banc One	17372	Chemical	60564			Corestate	14595		
104189	Bk. of America	Huntington	7718	Barnett	20229	Security Pacific	62606			NBD BancCorp.	21176		
		Crestar Finl.	9413	NCNB	27472	Chase	94766			Suntrust	26166		
		Signet	9471	Wells Fargo	44577					First Union	26820		
		US BancCorp.	9491							PNC Finl.	26936		
		MNC Finl.	9513							Bk. of Boston	34045		
		Valley Natl.	10716							Frst. Interstate	55422		
		Southeast	12469										
		Natl. City	14107										
		First Fidelity	15170										
		Wachovia	18690										
		Bk. of NE	22473										
AGGREGATE 313659			177088		186448		237647		385196		244519		51903

Figure 5.5

STRATEGIC GROUP MAP OF THE U.S. BANKING INDUSTRY (1987)

GROUP 1 BANK	ASSETS ($MM)	GROUP 2 BANK	ASSETS ($MM)	GROUP 3 BANK	ASSETS ($MM)	GROUP 4 BANK	ASSETS ($MM)	GROUP 5 BANKS	ASSETS ($MM)	GROUP 6 BANK	ASSETS ($MM)
Banponce Corp.	5390	Equimark	3140	First City TX	11202	Riggs Natl.	6788	Republic NY	22338	NCNB	28915
INB Finl.	5459	First Sec. UT	5074	Mellon	30525	State Street	6955	Continental	32391		
Marshall & Ill.	5556	First Empire	5177	Frt. Interstate	50927	Northern Trust	9326	First Chicago	44209		
First Maryland	5644	Commerce Banc	5269			Security Pacific	72838	Bankers Trust	56521		
Old Kent	6445	United Bk. CO	5503			Chemical	78189	Manny Hanny	73348		
Society Corp.	9077	First TN Natl.	5762			Chase	99133	J.P. Morgan	75414		
Manf. Natl.	9077	Mercantile	6766					Bk. of America	92833		
Comerica	10116	Firstar	7257					CitiCorp.	203607		
UJB Finl.	10139	AmSouth	7527								
KeyCorp.	11596	Dominion	7602								
Centrust	15036	Michigan Natl.	8481								
Bk. of NY	23065	Baybanks	8506								
NBD Bk. Corp.	23354	Huntington	8836								
First Bk. Sys.	26850	Crestar Finl.	9740								
Suntrust	27188	Ameritrust	10334								
First Union	27360	Signet	10724								
Bk. of Boston	34117	Valley Natl.	11300								
PNC Finl.	36504	Southeast	12842								
		US Bk. Corp.	13353								
		Natl. City	14912								
		MNC Finl.	16658								
		Bank One	18730								
		Wachovia	19342								
		Norwest	20747								
		C&S Sovran	21234								
		Fleet/Norstar	24531								
		Shawmut	26477								
		First Fidelity	28850								
		Bk. of NE	29475								
		Wells Fargo	44183								
AGGREGATE	291973		418332		92654		273229		600711		28915

Figure 5.6: Strategic Group Map Of The U.S. Banking Industry (1988)

Tier I RE Oriented Regs. — Bank	Assets ($MM)	Div. Regionals — Bank	Assets ($MM)	Bank	Assets ($MM)	Global Multirisk — Bank	Assets ($MM)	Trust Banking — Bank	Assets ($MM)
INB Finl.	5927	Equimark	3353	MNC Finl.	18015	Riggs Natl.	7002	State Street	8372
First Maryland	6274	First Sec. UT	5159	Midlantic	19697	Republic NY	24519		
Marshall & Ils.	6775	Commerce Banc	5444	Natl. City	21623	Continental	30578		
Old Kent	7854	Banponce Corp.	5707	Norwest	21750	First Chicago	44432		
Manf. Natl.	9331	United Bks. CO	5812	Wachovia	21815	Bankers Trust	57942		
Society Corp.	10010	First Empire	5908	C&S Sovran	22484	Manny Hanny	66710		
Ameritrust	10738	First TN Natl.	5972	Banc One	25274	J.P. Morgan	83923		
UJB Finl.	10888	Mercantile	6459	Barnett	25748	Bk. of America	94647		
Comerica	11146	Firstar	7842	Shawmut	28414	Chase Manhattan	97455		
KeyCorp.	14646	AmSouth	8313	Fleet/Norstar	29052	CitiCorp.	207666		
Corestates	16431	Dominion	9208	First Fidelity	29777				
NBD BanCorp.	24176	Baybanks	9496	Bk. of NE	32200				
First Bk. Sys.	24248	Huntington	9506	PNC Financial	40811				
First Union	28978	Meridian	9523	Wells Fargo	46617				
Suntrust	29177	Northern Trust	9904	Chemical	67349				
Mellon	31153	Crestar Finl.	10408	Security Pacific	77870				
Bk. of Boston	36061	Signet	11002						
Bk. of NY	47388	Michigan Natl.	11306						
First Interstate	58194	Valley Natl.	11766						
		First City TX	12196						
		US BanCorp.	14383						
		Southeast	15623						
AGGREGATE	389395				752634		714874		8372

GROUP 1 BANK	ASSETS ($ MM)	GROUP 2 BANK	ASSETS ($ MM)	GROUP 3 BANK	ASSETS ($ MM)	GROUP 4 BANK	ASSETS ($ MM)	GROUP 5 BANK	ASSETS ($ MM)
Valley Natl.	10551	State Street	11651	US BanCorp	17613	Continental	27143	Southeast	13390
Signet	11405	Northern Trust	11789	First Bk. Sys.	19001	Mellon	28762	Midlantic	23586
Meridian	11866	Society Corp.	15110	Key Corp.	19266	Fleet/Norstar	32507	Shawmut	23703
Boatmen's Banc	17469	Corestates	23520	Natl. City	23743	PNC Finl.	45534	MNC Finl.	26376
Barnett Bk.	32214	Wachovia	26271	First Fidelty	29110	NCNB	65285	Fst. Interstate	51357
Bk. of Boston	32529	NBD BanCorp	26747	First Union	40781	Security Pacific	84731		
Bk. of NY	45390	Republic NY	29597	Bk. of America	110728	CitiCorp	216986		
First Chicago	50779	Banc One	30336						
C&S Sovran	51238	Norwest	30626						
Manny Hanny	61530	Suntrust	33411						
Chemical Bk.	73019	Wells Fargo	56199						
Chase	98064	Bankers Trust	63596						
		J.P. Morgan	93103						
AGGREGATE	495054		451956		260242		500948		138412

Figure 5.7: Resource Based Strategic Group Map Of The U.S. Banking Industry

Notes

1. It is recognized that due to impact of excluded variables, there is a serial correlation between the error term and dependent variable, which leads to the presence of seemingly unrelated regressions (Johnston, 1972; Zellner 1962). Thus it would be more appropriate to perform a GLS regression instead of OLS to improve the efficiency of parameters. Unfortunately, GLS procedure is not available in the SPSS software package, and given the fact that we were interested only in the nature and not the strength of association, the complexity and time involved in transferring files to another software program did not justify performing a GLS regression. In general, the results from the two procedures are quite similar (Cool and Schendel 1988).

Chapter VI
Discussion of Results

In this chapter the empirical results relating to the four research questions and their associated hypotheses are discussed and analyzed in the context of the U.S. banking industry. An attempt is made to integrate the findings and discussion with the existing strategic group research and draw the comparative as well as the unique implications of this study for strategic management research in general and the strategic groups stream in particular.

6.1 RESEARCH QUESTION 1

What are the dynamic patterns of strategic group formation and movement over a period of time? What is the impact of discontinuous environmental change on inter group mobility and firm risk return relationships?

This question really is composed of two separate parts. They are discussed separately. The first part does not lend itself to formal hypotheses testing, therefore a comparative descriptive approach is employed for its analysis. Two previous studies: the pharmaceutical industry study by Cool (1985), and the insurance industry study by Fiegenbaum (1987), which performed more or less similar longitudinal analysis are used for comparing the changes in competitive patterns in the banking industry with other industries. However, it should be noted that this study employed a methodologically superior clustering algorithm, and used a highly rigorous and industry grounded variable specification procedure.

6.1.1 Dynamic Patterns of Strategic Group Formation

Strategic group dynamics are associated with three kind of changes: a change in group strategy, a change in the number of groups and a change in group membership. As discussed in chapter three, change in group strategy is captured by the methodology employed for identification of SSTPs. An analysis of competitive patterns in the banking industry from 1974-88 indicated that the fifteen year period was characterized by six sub-periods of varying duration in which strategic groups changed their strategy.

Cool found four sub-periods of seven, five, four, and three years duration from 1963-82 in pharmaceutical industry, while Fiegenbaum found nine sub-periods (five single year, and four double year) from 1970-84 in the insurance industry. The pattern of declining length of SSTPs observed in this study is similar to Cool's study, while the presence of single year time periods parallels Fiegenbaum's findings in the insurance industry.

A central debate in strategic management concerns the role of exogenous environmental changes versus endogenous strategic choice initiatives in triggering strategic change (Mascarenhas, 1989). Although the methodology employed to identify stable sub-periods within fifteen year study horizons, was statistical, its corroboration by significant preceding industry events as detailed in table 5.1, enhances the validity of the procedure. At the same time, it lends support to the environmental determinism perspective which contends that environmental shifts drive strategy changes that may result in changes in group strategy. This issue is further explored in the discussion of impact of discontinuous change on inter-group mobility. A discussion of the changes in number of strategic groups and firm membership - the other two types of strategic group dynamics follows next.

The number of existing strategic groups changed from one period to next. In the period before deregulation, four strategic groups were identified as characterizing strategic asymmetry in the banking industry. This number increased to five and six respectively in the next two time periods which coincided with two successive deregulation initiatives. In the fourth time period maximum strategic heterogeneity was observed as the number of strategic groups went up to seven, before shrinking to five and four respectively in the last two time periods.

Despite these dynamic changes in the strategic group structure, three core strategic patterns seemed to characterize competition in the banking industry over the entire study horizon. These are the global multirisk group, the diversified regionals group, and the real estate oriented tier I regionals. This lends support to Fiegenbaum and Thomas's speculation that "there are long-term structural equilibria in terms of strategic group positions, but that, in the short term, environmental discontinuities, disturbances, and strategic repositionings create the need to search for new, more sustainable competitive positions" (1990:212).

In terms of firm mobility, a high degree of membership change was observed between each time period, as firms attempted to reposition themselves to take advantage of the perceived opportunities afforded by deregulation, as also to learn about their comparative strategic advantages. This behavior can be attributed to both strategic change and strategic adjustment (Snow & Hambrick, 1980). Huntington's fundamental decision to move from wholesale banking to retail banking is an illustration of strategic change, while Chase's move to trust banking in 1986 and 1987 and its return to the global group and Chemical's constant repositioning are examples of short term strategic adjustment.

Finally, some strategic groups witnessed a greater membership stability than others. As can be observed from figures 5.1 to 5.6, the global group was fairly stable across time periods except for 1986. A notable stability was also observed in the diversified regional group. This may be due to superior mobility barriers protecting these groups which prevent entry into the group, while at their same acting as exit barriers for incumbents within the group.

A comparison of these results with Cool (1985) and Fiegenbaum (1987), suggests similarities in the dynamic pattern of group formation. First, as in the pharmaceutical industry, the banking industry returned to its original number of strategic groups after having undergone a structural transformation. However, an important distinction exists in that while Cool found six, five, four and six groups in the four time periods, i.e. a reduction in strategic asymmetry before returning to the original level, this study found exactly the opposite - an increase in strategic asymmetry before reverting to the original number.

Second, as in the insurance industry (Fiegenbaum (1987), three core positions seemed to persist over the entire fifteen year period. A similar finding was reported by Lewis and Thomas (1990) and Mascarenhas (1989). Third, a high degree of firm mobility and differential membership stability of strategic groups is consistent with Cool's findings. Cool attributed this firm mobility to a leader-follower phenomenon, where the strategic group members followed the strategy change of the firm altering its strategy first. In the banking industry some sort of a "herd mentality" is clearly apparent, where the firms changed groups more on a adhoc and nonsystematic basis, thereby making it difficult to establish a leader-follower phenomenon.

This may be because as opposed to the pharmaceutical industry, no clear cut leaders exist in the banking industry. In fact, most innovation in the banking industry comes from outside the industry, since the industry boundaries are fluid, while the pharmaceutical industry is very well defined. Theoretical and empirical exploration of the apparent differences between firm mobility patterns in these two studies, is a promising avenue for future research.

In general the patterns of strategic group formation and change observed in this study are more similar to the insurance industry, than to the pharmaceutical industry. This suggests that the strategic group structure in service industries (both banking and insurance are service businesses) may be different from manufacturing industries[1].

Relating these findings to the questions of existence and stability of strategic groups outlined at the beginning of the study, the following observations can be made. First, since strategic groups persisted during the entire fifteen year period of this study, it can be inferred that strategic groups are not a random phenomenon in the U.S. banking industry. Further, the fact that strategic groups were found both before and after deregulation - two very different competitive contexts, shows that strategic groups generically characterize competition, thereby lending support to Fiegenbaum and Thomas assertion that "strategic groups are a relatively stable, integral characteristic of industry structure" (1990: 212). The correspondence of the statistically derived groupings with the perceived natural groupings in this industry (this is discussed below) lends further weight to this statement.

Second, limited support is found for the stability of strategic groups. A longitudinal analysis of strategic groups revealed that although three core groups persisted over the fifteen year study period, changes in strategic group membership occurred quite frequently and the degree of membership stability differed across strategic groups. This finding is consistent with the results of both Cool (1985) and Fiegenbaum (1987), and is an expression of the dynamic aspects of competitive strategy (Cool, 1985). An alternative explanation, which questions the validity of employing scope and resource deployment variables for group identification, is advanced in the next chapter.

Before leaving the discussion of strategic group dynamics, one final point needs to made regarding the validity of the underlying clustering solutions. Thomas and Venkatraman (1988) have called for doing more confirmatory clustering rather than exploratory clustering. It is not clear however, as to what is gained by confirmatory clustering, other than establishing the robustness of the clustering algorithm. There is hardly anything interesting or enlightening about strategic groups which corroborate industry wisdom rather than complement it. Also not only is this clearly problematic in a longitudinal study, it may not be very desirable either, since the whole intent is to capture shifting strategic repositioning[2].

To the extent that the purpose of clustering is to validate the procedure itself, it is encouraging to note that the cluster solution of 1988, is very much in tune with the current industry wisdom, and was expected a priori. Most industry analysts recognize the banking industry to be composed of four major groups - the money center banks (comparable to global multirisk cluster), the super regionals (comparable to diversified regionals), the tier I regionals and the trust banks. The correspondence of the statistical results with the "real picture", should substantially enhance the validity of the findings and is indicative of the robustness of the results.

Left out of this scheme are the community banks which are not captured in this study due to the nature of the sample employed. Another apparent anomaly is the classification of Bank of America in the global banking group. Some industry analysts regard Bank of America as more of a super regional in its strategic makeup (Bryan, 1988). A similar finding was reported by Mehra (1990) in a pilot study.

This example raises an important conceptual point. Firms within a strategic group can differ in their strategic makeup, however usually they are more similar to each other than to firms in other groups. Although the group descriptions are based on cluster centroids, a more accurate picture is obtained by looking at group means and standard deviations which signify internal dispersion, simultaneously. In other words, a strategic group is akin to a "web", with firms in the group following similar but not exactly same strategies. This view permits firm level differences in the fine tuning of strategic postures rather than conceiving a strategic group as a "platter" with firms sitting on top of each other, and having congruent strategic configurations.

This concludes the descriptive analysis of the incidence of strategic groups, changes in number of strategic groups, and changes in strategic group membership for the U.S. Banking industry. Next, we turn our attention to understanding the impact of discontinuous environmental change on inter-group mobility and risk-return relationship.

6.1.2 Impact of Discontinuous Environment on Inter-Group Mobility

To assess the impact of environmental discontinuities on inter group mobility and strategic repositioning, it is important to distinguish between two very different kinds of environmental discontinuities, which seem to generate contrasting response patterns. The first occurred in 1980, leading to significant deregulation in the industry, and altering the competitive "rules of the game". To a large extent, this regulatory initiative was introduced to level the playing field between commercial banks and other financial institutions. It was anticipated, and considered desirable by the industry. I label this change process as benevolent change.

The second discontinuity occurred in 1987 - the LDC debt crises. It was drastic, unprecedented, and almost unexpected. It threw the whole industry into state of chaos, and left a permanent scar on the industry's fiscal health. I label this change process as malevolent change. Both types of discontinuities led to increased inter-group mobility as suggested by hypothesis one, thereby, providing support for the "environmentalist" school of strategy researchers. However, while benevolent change seems to lead to increased strategic heterogeneity, malevolent change triggers a retraction and strategic homogeneity. Again, the pace of adaptation/change is slow for benevolent change, while it is rapid and adhoc for malevolent change. This can be seen by the fact that it took the industry seven years to achieve maximum strategic heterogeneity, reflecting a lagging response pattern to the opportunities afforded by deregulation, while it took it only two years to achieve a complete withdrawal/retraction in the face of LDC debt crises. Finally, it does appear that benevolent change encourages endogenous strategic initiatives, while malevolent change seems to stifle strategic choice initiatives.

The results do seem to suggest that benevolent change has an indirect effect on industry structure by promoting more endogenous strategic initiatives in the form of innovative and riskier strategies which in turn change the structure. Malevolent environmental change on the other hand, constitutes an exogenous shock which has a strong and a direct effect on altering the structure of industry. In other words, it appears that the nature of change moderates the relationship between industry structure, environment, and strategic choice. This then implies that environmental adaptation, and strategic choice perspectives should not be viewed as competing and mutually exclusive but as complementary. It appears that both perspectives can coexist and provide a richer and more accurate description when employed jointly rather than when employed separately.

6.1.3 Impact of Discontinuous Environment on Firm Level Risk-Return Relationship

The second hypothesized impact of environmental discontinuity was on the firm level risk-return relationships. A negative risk-return relationship was found to exist in the banking industry for the entire duration of the study. This finding is quite significant. While it adds cumulative evidence to the "risk-return paradox" in strategic management first uncovered by Armour and Teece (1978) and Bowman (1980), its rationale is a little different from existing explanations.

Bowman (1982) suggested that "risk-return paradox" exists due to what he called "troubled firms," which, because of their poor profitability, had to take large risks to improve their situation. On the other hand, Jemison (1987: 1087) noted that "risk and return may be tapping two different dimensions of performance." While Fiegenbaum and Thomas (1988) explained the paradox by employing a priori concepts from behavioral decision theory and prospect theory.

In their earlier work they (Fiegenbaum & Thomas, 1986) found that the risk-return paradox was dependent on the time period adopted in the study. It was more likely to hold in unpredictable and uncertain environments. This was consistent with Bowman (1980) who conjectured that regulated, and hence stable industries would be more likely to have positive risk-return relationships.

Cool and Schendel (1988) suggested that when environmental changes or discontinuities follow each other at a quick pace, they may prompt firms to alter their strategic behavior. This results in a negative risk-return relationship at the firm level which "rests on the assumption that both 'troubled' and 'successful' firms populate the same strategic group" (1988: 218). In their study of the pharmaceutical industry, they found a alternating risk return relationship, with the first two periods (1962-69 and 1970-74) having a positive relationship, while the last two periods (1975-79 and 1980-82) having a negative relationship. However, the beta coefficient in the third time period was not significant and in the fourth time period it was significant only at 15% level of confidence. Nevertheless, they noted that "the fact that negative risk-return relationships may persist over a long period of time suggests that industries may go through sustained phases of disequilibrium" (1988: 220).

It is debatable whether the banking industry has been in a state of disequilibrium over the entire fifteen period of this study. What is more likely is that beyond a certain level, negative risk-return relationship is built into the very nature of banking. In general, bank products (loans) are priced according to a positive risk-return calculus i.e. the riskier the loan, the higher the lending interest rate. But default on these risky loans can have a very debilitating effect on bank performance. And, since these defaults are unpredictable and follow a stochastic pattern, they increase the volatility of earnings - the variance of returns, thereby generating a negative risk-return function.

6.2 RESEARCH QUESTION 2

What is the nature of the relationship between strategic group membership and firm performance?

Both within and across group performance differences were investigated to address this question. I begin by discussing the across group differences first.

A multivariate analysis of variance, showed that strategic groups in the banking industry statistically differed in their economic performance levels at $p < .001$ level of significance in all the time periods. Risk differences were significant in five out of six time periods, while risk adjusted differences were significant only in 1988. These findings of economic and risk differences are consistent with Fiegenbaum (1987), but the finding of the risk adjusted differences in the last time period is at variance with existing research. Cool (1985) found differences only along the market share dimension of performance, and no differences in risk and risk adjusted levels.

At least two different explanations may be advanced for significant risk adjusted differences in the last time period. The first is that these differences may reflect a crystallization of industry structure as can seen by looking at the differences in the comparative distances between cluster centroids of the three core groups in the first and last time periods. (See table 6.1 below.) The distance between the cluster centroids of the global and diversified regional group has increased by 15% over a fifteen year period, the distance between diversified regional and tier I regionals has increased by 84%, while the distance between the global and tier I regionals has reduced by 29%. Overall a pattern of homogenization of comparative distances between the cluster centroids of the three core groups is noticeable.

Alternatively, it might be a random phenomenon caused by unusually strong performance numbers for the industry in this time period as discussed in chapter four. This assertion is supported by Dean and Amel's (1991) study which found that firm effects are subdued during periods of prosperity, thereby translating into lesser within groups variance, and thus resulting in stronger across group effects.

Table 6.1 Distances between cluster centroids of three core strategic groups

	1979 Global	Div. Reg.	1988 Global	Div. Reg.
Div. Reg.	38.82		44.72	
Tier I Reg.	45.20	17.52	31.88	32.18

A univariate analysis of performance however shows that differences for ROAA were significant in five out of six time periods, for PPE on four out of six, and for PE only in one time period. Differences on risk exposure in univariate tests were "mostly" non-significant. This has two implications: First, it suggests the importance of multiple measure operationalization and testing of performance. Since some of the measures individually (i.e. in the univariate tests) may not be significant, but in combination with others (i.e. in the MANOVA) they become significant. Only two other studies (Cool, 1985; Fiegenbaum, 1987) performed multivariate tests and found significant differences on the economic dimension of performance. It is tempting therefore, to speculate that over reliance on single measures and/or univariate tests may have contributed to the inconsistent findings of the previous research (e.g. Porter 1979, Oster, 1982, Frazier & Howell 1983, Dess & Davis 1984).

Second, the nonsignificance of financial market measures across most time periods may indicate that financial markets and analysts focus on individual firms rather than strategic groups. This would explain the high standard deviations on the PE measure. A similar phenomenon was also reported by Lewis and Thomas (1990: 395), who observed that "we find that PER varies more within than between groups, suggesting that markets and analysts analyze individual firms".

The finding of differential risk levels across groups suggests that Cool and Schendel's (1988) conclusion that risk differences exist only at the firm level may be premature. The argument for group level risk differences is supported by similar empirical findings by Fiegenbaum and Thomas (1990) and the theoretical arguments advanced by Caves and Porter (1977), to the effect that investments in mobility barriers are inherently risky.

Finally, while Cool and Schendel (1987) found that performance differences across groups are not significant in periods with lower strategic asymmetry, this study finds exactly the opposite i.e., performance differences between groups are more significant in periods with lower strategic asymmetry. It therefore follows that structural characteristics need to be explicitly considered in strategy-performance studies, as suggested by Cool & Schendel (1987).

A longitudinal analysis of performance levels associated with each strategic group indicated that the diversified regionals and trust banking group consistently outperformed all other groups in the industry. These two strategic groups roughly correspond to Porter's cost leadership and focused differentiation strategies. This suggests that not all generic strategies are equally viable, in the banking industry (Wright 1984). A similar result was reported by Cool (1985), who found that a strategy of differentiation was superior to every other posture in the pharmaceutical industry. In the present context, the global group is the closest in its orientation to the differentiation strategy. It is also the group protected by the highest mobility barriers, and thus, would be expected to outperform every other group in the industry (Caves & Porter, 1977). Its inferior performance, therefore, is quite surprising.

At least two different explanations may be advanced for this phenomenon. The first is that the underlying commodity nature of the product makes it very difficult to create a differentiated image, and if created it may be difficult to recover the costs of differentiating through premium pricing. Differentiation in the banking industry appears to be viable only if it is targeted to a particular segment or niche (e.g.trust banking). Otherwise, industry economics favor low cost producers.

The second reason for the inferior performance of the globals may be differential intra-group rivalry. The diversified regionals lack market interpenetration, as their primary markets are pretty well staked out and delineated. Globals, on the other hand, have a high degree of market interdependence, are intensely rivalrous, and face competition from foreign banks and "non-banks". Therefore, the favorable protective effects of mobility barriers are competed away by high intra-group rivalry. This explanation for "high barriers but low performance" syndrome is different from the "mobility barriers becoming exit barriers" explanation advanced by Mascarenhas and Aaker (1989).

In sum, the presence of economic and risk differences across strategic groups means that strategic postures in the banking industry vary in their attendant riskiness. But, the lack of risk adjusted differences directs our attention to the within group performance differences, and hence, to the differential set of skills and assets of the firms.

Differences in performance among firms following similar strategies can exist because of at least three reasons. First, the differential set of resource endowments of individual firms creates a difference between firms in their ability to execute their chosen strategy. Second, while all firms in a strategic group follow similar strategy, some firms may pursue it more vigorously than others (Cool, 1985). Third, some firms may have recently entered the group, and therefore, may be adjusting to the new strategy. Whatever the causes, the significant within group differences found here, put a burden on future strategic groups research to investigate both within and across group performance differences.

It is important, however, to realize that both within and across group performance differences put together will not necessarily soak the entire intraindustry performance variance. Performance is a slippery concept and although explaining variance in performance (within and across industries) is at the heart of strategic management research, future strategic group researchers should bear in mind that group-performance linkage can be tempered by a number (such as differential inter and intra group rivalry, business cycles etc.) of controllable and noncontrollable factors. Thus while in some industries a direct linkage between groups and performance may be hard to establish, nevertheless an indirect linkage may exist.

6.3 RESEARCH QUESTION 3

Does the gap between capabilities and strategy account for firm performance differences?

It is now generally recognized at least theoretically, in strategy research that firm performance is influenced by a host of firm-specific and market-specific factors (Porter, 1979; Hansen & Wernerfelt 1989). However, empirical research has largely failed to capture the complexity of firm level performance determinants, perhaps due to the difficulty of obtaining data on firm capabilities. This question was directed at modeling the firm performance relationship in more a complex fashion. It also served as a bridge/transition point between research question two and four which explore two contrasting models of strategic group formation and attendant performance linkages.

The results show that firm capabilities added significantly to the explanation of firm performance on all three dimensions of performance - profitability (ROAA), productivity (PPE), and ability to generate resources (PE). The percentage of variance explained for 1988 (R^2) however, is quite low. As discussed in chapter V, this may be attributed to 1988 being an unusually profitable year for the industry, resulting in a lot of noise in the relationship. The contribution of strategic group membership and firm capabilities is roughly equal.

This picture changes dramatically if 1990 (a relatively normal year) performance figures are used. The overall variance explained jumps by about 300% for ROAA, about 70% for PPE and about 120% for PE. Interestingly, most of this variance is accounted for by firm capabilities. This could reflect two things. First it suggests the increasing importance of firm capabilities as competitive and rent generating weapons in the banking industry. Second, it also suggests that strategic group structure in 1990 is likely to have changed markedly from 1988, and hence the low R^2 for 1988 strategic group membership when used as a predictor for 1990 firm performance. This dramatic shift also highlights the pitfalls of imputing premature causality based on the results of a cross-sectional study.

These results provide an empirical test of Cool and Schendel's (1988) conjecture that performance differences within strategic groups may be attributed to differences in firm asset endowment. They are also consistent with findings of Hansen and Wernerfelt (1989) who using a different research design and investigative framework found that both economic and organization factors are highly significant predictors of firm performance, but that organizational factors explain more variance than economic factors.

Further, similar to their findings, this study finds that strategic group membership and firm capabilities are orthogonal and thus independent contributors to firm performance. The lack of interaction between these set of factors suggests that these two perspectives are supplementary rather than complementary as argued by Hansen and Wernerfelt (1989).

Finally, although the R^2 in this study (using 1990 numbers) is higher than Hansen & Wernerfelt's (1989) integrated model (their R^2 was .457), a substantial portion of the variance in intra industry performance differences is still unexplained. This may be explained by looking at following hierarchy of performance determinants summarized by Porter (1979: 219):

> "The structure within an industry consists of its configuration of strategic groups, including their mobility barriers, size and composition, strategic distance, and market interdependence relative to each other. The firm will have higher profits if it is located in a group with the best combination of high mobility barriers, insulation from intergroup rivalry and substitute products, bargaining power with adjacent industries, the fewest other members, and suitability to the firm's execution ability".

Thus although strategic group membership and firm capabilities are meaningful predictors of firm performance, a variety of other factors such as competitive intensity can also influence performance. This suggests that future research should employ complex models which include multiple predictors to fully capture the multifaceted nature of firm performance determinants.

6.4 RESEARCH QUESTION 4

Are firm resource bundles better predictors of strategic group membership than observed product market strategies?

An analysis of this question involved first identifying strategic groups based on key resources, and then comparing them with the strategic groups based on positioning strategies, in order to ascertain the differences in the group membership structure and the relative ability to explain performance variation. Such a comparison however is inherently limited, since the sample composition and temporal horizon of the two designs - the longitudinal one used to identify product market strategy based groups, and the cross-sectional one used to identify resource based groups, are quite different.

A closer examination reveals that at least two mediating factors prevent this comparison from being as flawed as it may first appear. First, forty four out of the forty five banks in the cross-sectional sample (as pointed out in chapter V, Meridian Bancorp. is the only exception) are included in longitudinal sample of sixty eight banks. Thus, the cross-sectional sample is really a subset of the longitudinal sample. Furthermore, the fact that a substantial degree of robustness was observed in the underlying strategic group structure of the longitudinal sample when clustering was performed on a reduced set of firms, should inspire confidence in direct comparison of the two models.

Second, although data on firm resources was collected in the summer of 1991, while the temporal horizon of positioning variables does not extend beyond 1988, the fact that firm resources are accumulated over a period of time, and hence are more durable, should enhance the meaningfulness of contrasting the two approaches. Nevertheless, the findings of this research question and its associated hypotheses should be treated as strictly exploratory, as was pointed in the introductory chapter.

Despite the design limitations, the novelty of this approach to operationalizing firm capabilities and its significance for future strategic groups research can be appreciated by examining the following statement made by Collis (1991: 50) in defense of using the case based method for an resource based analysis of global bearings industry:

> "While a case study has its drawbacks, at this stage
> in the development of the resource-based analysis of the
> firm it is only appropriate methodology (Montgomery,

1990). The need for a fine-grained analysis inside the firm prevents a broader sample study, and the lack of standardized measures of the important concepts inhibits statistical analysis"

The finding of a substantially higher explanatory power of resource based groups as opposed to product-market based groups is quite suggestive, and points to a fruitful avenue for future research. Combining these results with the theoretical arguments advanced in chapter two, a prima facie case appears to exist for employing resource based variables as the primary group defining variables in future strategic groups studies.

The presence of J.P. Morgan and Banc One - two banks which are generally perceived as having very different banking strategies, with Morgan being essentially a wholesale bank and Banc One being a retail bank suggests three things: First, it appears that there may be two levels of competition in an industry; the primary level where firms compete for key input resources and the secondary level where they compete for customers. This implies that it is possible for a firm to have two different set of competitors. For example, Morgan and Banc One compete at the primary level for a limited amount of banking talent, for capital, for technological expertise etc. However, at the secondary level, Morgan probably competes more with CitiCorp. for asset growth, while Banc One competes with National City or Society Corp. for retail deposits and mortgage origination.

Second, drawing on the distinction between actual competition and potential competition from contestability theory, it is tempting to speculate that while these two players are not actual rivals in the most market segments at point in time, this does not preclude them from invading each others markets in future. This may be accomplished either through direct entry or by buying up each other's competition, given the fact that they are both well endowed with strategic resources. In fact, such a phenomenon is already observable in the industry, as it continues its relentless move towards nationwide banking, with the recent dramatic upturn in the merger and consolidation activity.

Thus, these two banks are potential competitors. It would be very fruitful for future research to build a predictive model of rivalry based on these resource based groups. For instance an interesting question would be whether mergers would occur between firms in the same group or across groups, and if so between what groups. This would enable us to address the theoretical question of whether resource complementerties are more important than resource additions, or in other words, is there a point beyond which the marginal value of accumulating a certain strategic resources is zero.

Third, it points to the fungibility of certain core resources like technological expertise which can be deployed in very different fashions. Again, while Morgan uses its high degree of technological expertise for developing hedging and currency trading programs, Banc One uses its considerable technological prowess to maintain efficient back office operations, detailed data bases on individual customers, and providing real time information to bank employees.

Finally an careful inspection of figure 5.7 and table 5.15 illustrate two other important points for the emerging resource based view of the firm. First, without scope/positioning variables, it is hard to describe resource based groups. The basic nature of the resource based view is very inward looking. It makes a fundamental assumption that a firm will automatically deploy its resources in the most appropriate environments (markets, segments, niches, etc.). The strength of this assumption remains to be empirically tested. For the present, it does appear that some positioning variables are required to describe different strategy types. Whether positioning variables/strategies are redundant except for purely descriptive purposes is question that future research needs to address.

Second, consistent with the theoretical arguments advanced in chapter two, a comparison of group two with group four shows that of themselves skill have little value, but in combination with suitable assets their value enhancing potential goes up dramatically. This is illustrated by the fact that while both groups two and four are strong on skills such as technological expertise, innovation capability, and placing power, group two has a stronger capital base and higher quality assets, and consequently outperforms group four.

This concludes the discussion of the four research questions and the implications of the findings for the strategic group research in particular and the strategic management research in general. Next, I summarize the findings of this study and highlight the theoretical and methodological contributions of this study to strategic management, and its implications for the banking industry.

Notes

1. For a detailed theoretical exploration of the relationship between industry stucture and strategic group characteristics, see Mehra and Floyd (1992).

2. I do appreciate the underlying spirit of Thomas and Venkatraman's (1988) call, though, which is to combine more industry understanding with methodological rigor in performing strategic groups analysis, particularly given the fact that most extant research has been "data-driven" (Mcgee and Thomas, 1986).

Chapter VII
Conclusions

This study traced the patterns of competition, strategic orientations, and the differential risk/return profiles associated with various business strategies in the banking industry. It addressed the unresolved questions of strategic groups existence, stability, and performance effects by examining two contrasting models of strategic group formation/identification.

The study found that strategic groups characterized competition in the banking industry both before and after deregulation. Some support was found for the underlying stability of the strategic groups, despite the profound changes characterizing the banking industry. Environmental discontinuity was found to enhance inter-group mobility and strengthen the negative risk-return relationship prevalent in this industry. Across group performance differences were found on economic and risk dimensions, but not on risk-adjusted dimensions except in the last time period. Within group performance differences were highly significant but in over half the cases, risk differences within groups were non-significant. Firm capabilities were found to be much better predictors of intraindustry performance variation than strategic group membership, although both were significant predictors in their own right. Finally, resource based groupings appeared to be a empirically viable representation of industry rivalry and these groups were meaningful predictors of economic performance.

The combination of exogenous discontinuities (environment) and endogenous imitation/distancing activities, seemed to have functioned as powerful forces in upsetting the structural equilibria in the banking industry. This structural transformation seems to have quickened with the passage of time, due to weakening mobility barriers in the banking industry.

Although given the commodity nature of the underlying product, positioning variables do not perhaps constitute strong mobility barriers to begin with, the erosion of their strength has been facilitated by the development of secondary and derivative financial markets. The emergence of these markets has created a tremendous degree of substitutability/liquidity of the strategic asset investments. Therefore, a change in strategy merely requires a change in the portfolio mix, given the high degree of factor mobility. For example, a bank can sell its mortgage portfolio or its credit card portfolio in the secondary markets for asset based securities or to quasi-government bodies such as Fannie Mae, thereby exiting the consumer loans market. This relative flexibility of the asset portfolio makes scope and resource deployment variables to be very fluid dimensions of strategy in the banking industry.

This observation leads one to speculate that for financial services industry in particular and for service industries in general, strategic groups should be identified by using skill based measures which provide more durable mobility barriers. Furthermore, the ability of capability variables to explain substantial percentage of intra-industry performance heterogeneity suggests that the bases of competitive advantage for service businesses may be different from manufacturing businesses.

Next I summarize the theoretical and methodological contributions of this study for strategic management research and its implications for the banking industry.

7.1 THEORETICAL AND EMPIRICAL CONTRIBUTIONS TO STRATEGIC MANAGEMENT RESEARCH

The major contribution of this study lies in extending the strategic groups literature by combining it with the resource based view of the firm to advance a resource based model of strategic groups and empirically testing this proposition by showing these groups indeed do have a strong predictive validity. Thus, conceptually it made a case for redefining the focus of strategic groups research to include resource based variables as primary group defining variables, since they are more durable sources of mobility barriers.

Second, although tangential to the focus of this study, the analysis revealed some interesting implications for the resource based view of the firm. Rather than just talking about rare, valuable and nonsubsitutable resources, the study empirically identified a set of ten key resources in the banking industry. Of course, a further a micro level fine tuning of individual resources is possible. Further, it appears that certain configurations of resources are superior to others. Thus, simply being endowed with or developing resources which provide competitive advantage is not enough, unless they are deployed in suitable combinations. This configuration approach may strengthen the resource based view in adding to our understanding of intraindustry heterogeneity. Additionally, it appears that the implicit assumption of appropriate deployment of resources in the most suitable product market strategy arenas made by the resource based view is not empirically tenable.

Third, the study proposed and tested a expanded model of strategy-performance linkage by including firm resource endowments along with strategic group membership to explain intra-industry performance heterogeneity. This model acts as a sort of bridge or a transition mechanism between the traditional product market strategy based conceptualization of strategic groups and the alternative resource based model of strategic groups proposed in this study. However, while this model does have a higher explanatory power, a substantial proportion of the performance variation was still unexplained, suggesting that strategic management research needs to move away from simplistic notions of performance-strategy linkage.

Fourth, the study reinforced the findings of earlier single industry studies by showing that strategic groups characterize competition in two very different competitive contexts. Performance differences existed both across and within strategic groups, thus confirming that strategic group membership does indeed have a linkage with both performance and risk, albeit a limited one. Although this was only the second study to investigate both within and across group differences, it does seem that it is time to close the debate on the predictive validity of strategic groups. Performance differences can exist both across and within groups, with extent of these differences being moderated by the structural context of the industry.

Fifth, it was shown that risk differences can exist at both the group and firm level, as opposed to Cool and Schendel's (1988) assertion that they exist only at the firm level. It was argued that their conclusion may be premature. Theoretical arguments were made to back the empirical findings. Thus, for a fuller understanding of the strategy-performance relationship, future research should investigate risk differences at both group and the firm level.

Sixth, it added to the growing body of empirical research in strategic management (Bowman, 1980; Fiegenbaum & Thomas 1986 etc.) on risk-return paradox by showing that negative risk-return function can exist in certain industries due to the structural nature of these industries. This is at variance with the explanations of instability (Bowman, 1980) and prospect theory (Fiegenbaum & Thomas, 1986), advanced in the existing research.

Finally, the study showed that discontinuous change has a profound effect on industry structure and risk-return calculus, but that the relationship between environment and strategy is moderated by the nature of change itself. Research on strategic change is concerned with understanding both the content/magnitude and the process of change (Ginsberg, 1988), or delineating the differences between strategic change and strategic adjustment (Snow & Hambrick, 1980). Previous research has largely focused on investigating the role of strategic choice, environmental adaptation, or population ecology perspectives in accounting for strategic change (Mascarenhas, 1989) without looking at the type of change itself. This study extended this stream of literature by adding a new dimension to it.

7.2 METHODOLOGICAL CONTRIBUTIONS

The resource based view of the firm is gaining increasing prominence in strategic management research. Ghoshal and Bartlett (1991) have referred to it as a exciting new paradigm which has the potential to pull diverse strands of strategy research under a unifying umbrella. However, a critical impediment in the development of this view has been the difficulty encountered in operationalizing firm levels skills/capabilities and testing their significance in a positivist framework. This study develops and tests a novel approach to resolve the knotty issue of measuring firm level skills that is compatible with large sample research.

Second, while multiple measures of performance have been used in some of the recent strategic groups studies (Cool & Schendel, 1987; Fiegenbaum & Thomas 1990; Lewis & Thomas 1991) measurement of strategic (i.e. firms' long term health and adaptation capability) as opposed to economic performance (historical picture) is a novelty in this research stream. Third, this is the first longitudinal strategic groups study which employed market based measures of performance along with accounting based measures to comprehensively test the strategy-performance linkage.

Fourth, since the correct identification of strategic groups is critically dependent on the underlying clustering algorithm, this study employed a more robust two stage clustering algorithm, which overcomes the methodological weaknesses of hierarchical clustering. The benefit of this approach can be seen by the fact that in the last two time periods, second stage clustering reduced the number of clusters by one in each case. Further, multiple methods (scree tests, discriminant analysis, MANOVA, and sensitivity analysis) were employed to identify the correct number of clusters.

Finally, the explicit involvement of industry experts at each phase of this study, led to a grounded and rigorous variable specification. Again, the corroboration of statistically derived sub-periods with significant industry events is a first in this research stream and should substantially enhance the validity of the findings.

7.3 IMPLICATIONS FOR THE BANKING INDUSTRY

The primary import of this theses for bankers is the need to shift their strategic focus from privileged product market positions as basis for competitive advantage to the creating, nurturing, and sustaining key resources to enhance their long term competitive health. A list of ten such resources was identified in this study. This shift in focus also calls for supplementing their existing mental models of competition to include competitors in the primary market for resource accumulation, who are often not their competitors in product markets.

Another implication is that risk management is a core skill in the banking industry. Simply investing in state-of-art technological systems and financial engineering departments/products, will not be effective unless management has the depth and the vision to properly deploy these resources. Along with management quality, asset quality and a strong capital base are also very important in creating long term sustainable competitive advantage.

Finally, it appears that the strategic logic of this industry favors either low cost producers or highly focused competitors. Rewards from following a differentiated strategic posture are not commensurate with the incremental costs associated with going down that route. This suggests that management should focus on lowering its fixed cost base, uncovering hidden cross-subsidization among product lines, dropping non-viable products from the portfolio, and in general attending to cost control on an ongoing basis.

This is exemplified by the following observation about Cincinnati based highly successful Fifth Third Bancorp.: "The focus has been on efficiency and productivity; they count paper clips and figure customers don't care if there are no original oil paintings on the walls." (Wall Street Journal, 1992). For the present and in the near term, it does seem that "back to the basics" strategy is a clear winner in this industry. This situation may change, however as the industry consolidates and enters into some kind of long term dynamic equilibrium.

APPENDIX: RATING SHEET

Bank Name _____ Rater Code _____

1) Management Quality and Depth

|---------|---------|---------|---------|---------|---------|---------|---------|---------|
Low   Average   High

2) Franchise

|---------|---------|---------|---------|---------|---------|---------|---------|---------|
Low   Average   High

3) Asset/Credit Quality

|---------|---------|---------|---------|---------|---------|---------|---------|---------|
Low   Average   High

4) Technological Expertise

|---------|---------|---------|---------|---------|---------|---------|---------|---------|
Low   Average   High

5) Placing Power

|---------|---------|---------|---------|---------|---------|---------|---------|---------|
Low   Average   High

6) Adequacy of Capital Base

|---------|---------|---------|---------|---------|---------|---------|---------|---------|
Low   Average   High

7) Resource Management/Efficiency

|---------|---------|---------|---------|---------|---------|---------|---------|---------|
Low   Average   High

8) Innovation

|---------|---------|---------|---------|---------|---------|---------|---------|---------|
Low   Average   High

9) Risk Management

|---------|---------|---------|---------|---------|---------|---------|---------|---------|
Low   Average   High

10) Information Advantage/Asymmetry

|---------|---------|---------|---------|---------|---------|---------|---------|---------|
Low   Average   High

Bibliography

Aaker David A. "Managing Assets and Skills : The Key to Sustainable Competitive Advantage." *California Management Review.* Winter 1989. pp. 91-106.

Armour, H.O. & Teece, D.J. "Organizational Structure and Economic Performance: A Test of the Multidivisional Hypothesis." *Bell Journal of Economics.* 9, 1978. pp. 106-122.

Bain, J.S. *Barriers to New Competition.* Harvard University Press, Cambridge, Mass., 1956.

Barney Jay B. "Strategic Factors Markets: Expectations, Luck, and Business Strategy." *Management Science.* Vol. 32, No. 10, 1986. pp. 1231-1241.

Barney Jay B. "Asset Stocks and Sustained Competitive Advantage: A Comment." *Management Science.* Vol. 35, No. 12, 1989. pp. 1511.

Barney Jay B. & Hoskissen R.B. "Strategic Groups: Untested Assertions and Research Proposals." *Managerial and Decision Economics.* March 1990.

Barney, J.B. "Firm Resources and Sustained Competitive Advantage." *Journal of Management.* 17, 1991. pp. 99-120.

Bartlett, C.A. & Ghoshal, S. "Global Strategic Management: Impact on the New Frontiers of Strategy Research." *Strategic Management Journal.* Vol. 12, 1991. pp. 5-16.

Bettis, R.A. "Performance Differences in Related and Unrelated Diversified Firms." *Strategic Management Journal.* 2, 1981. pp. 379-393.

Biggadike, E.R. "The Contributions of Marketing to Strategic Management." *Academy of Management Review.* 6, 1981. pp. 621-32.

Bowman, E.H. "A Risk/Return Paradox for Strategic Management." *Sloan Management Review.* 21, Spring 1980. pp. 17-31.

Bowman, E.H. "Risk Seeking by Troubled Firms." *Sloan Management Review.* Summer 1982. pp. 33-40.

Bromiley, P. "Paradox or Least Variance Found: A Comment on 'Mean-Variance Approaches to Risk-Return Relationships in Strategy: Paradox Lost.'" *Management Science.* Vol. 37, No.9. September 1991. pp.1206-1210.

Brown, L.D. & Rozeff, M.S. "The Superiority of Analyst Forecasts as Measures of Expectations: Evidence from Earnings." *Journal of Finance.* 33, 1978. pp. 1-6.

Bryan, L.B. "Breaking up the Bank." Harper Collins, N.Y. 1988.

Caves, R.E. and M.E Porter. "From Entry Barriers to Mobility Barriers: Conjectural Decisions and Contrived Deterrence to New Competition." *Quarterly Journal of Economics.* 91, 1977. pp. 241-262.

Caves, R.E. "Industrial Organization, Corporate Strategy, and Structure: A Survey." *Journal of Economic Literature.* 18(1), 1980. pp. 64-92.

Caves, R.E. and Thomas Pugel. "Intra-Industry Differences in Conduct and Performance: Viable Strategies in U.S. Manufacturing Industries." New York University Monograph, 1980.

Caves, R.E. "Economic Analysis and the Quest for Competitive Advantage." *American Economic Review.* 74(2), 1984 pp. 127-132.

Christensen, H.K. & Montogemery C. "Corporate Economic Performance: Diversification Strategy Versus Market Structure." *Strategic Management Journal.* 1981. pp. 327-343.

Collins, D.J. "A Resource-Based Analysis of Global Competition: The Case of the Bearings Industry." *Strategic Management Journal.* Vol. 12, 1991. pp. 49-68.

Conant, J.S., M. P.Mokwa and P.R. Varadarajan. "Strategic Types, Distinctive Marketing Competencies and Organizational Performance: A Multiple Measures-Based Study." *Strategic Management Journal.* September 1990. pp. 365-384.

Cool, K. "Strategic Group Formation and Strategic Group Shifts: A Longitudinal Analysis of the U.S. Pharmaceutical Industry, 1963-1982." Ph.D. Dissertation. Purdue University, 1985.

Cool, K. and D. Schendel. "Strategic Group Formation and Performance: The Case of the U.S. Pharmaceutical Industry, 1963-1982." *Management Science.* 33(9), pp. 1-23.

Cool, K. and D. Schendel. "Performance Differences Among Strategic Group Members." *Strategic Management Journal,* 9(3), 1988. pp.207-223.

Dess, C.G. and P.S. Davis. "Porter's (1980) Generic Strategies as Determinants of Strategic Group Membership and Organizational Performance." *Academy of Management Journal.* 27, 1984. pp. 467-488.

Dierickx Ingemar and Cool K. "Asset Stock Accumulation and Sustainability of Competitive Advantage." *Management Science.* December 1989. pp. 1504-1513.

Everitt, B. *Cluster Analysis.* 2nd ed. New York: Halsted Press, 1980.

Fiegenbaum A., J. Mcgee and H. Thomas. "Exploring the Linkage Between Strategic Groups and Competitive Strategy."

International Studies of Management & Organization. Vol. XVIII, No.1, pp. 6-25.

Fiegenbaum, A. & Thomas, H. "Dynamic and Risk Measurement Perspectives on Bowman's Risk-Return Paradox for Strategic Management: An Empirical Study." *Strategic Management Journal.* 7, 1986. pp. 395-408.

Fiegenbaum, A. & Thomas, H. "Attitudes Toward Risk and the Risk-Return Paradox: Prospect Theory Explanations." *Academy of Management Journal.* 31(1), March 1988. pp. 85-106.

Fiegenbaum A. and H. Thomas. "Strategic Groups and Performance: The U.S. Insurance Industry, 1970-84." *Strategic Management Journal.* March-April 1990. pp. 197-216.

Gabel, L., "The Microfoundations of Competitive Strategy." Working Paper INSEAD. October 1984.

Galbraith, C. and D.E. Schendel. "An Empirical Analysis of Strategy Types." *Strategic Management Journal.* 4(2), 1983. pp. 153-173.

Ginsberg, A. "Measuring and Modelling Changes in Strategy: Theoretical Foundations and Empirical Directions." *Strategic Management Journal.* Vol. 9, 1988. pp. 559-575.

Grady, D.B. & A.H. Spencer. "Managing Commercial Banks: Community, Regional, and Global." Prentice Hall, N.J. 1990.

Green, P.E. *Analyzing Multivariate Data.* Hinsdale, Ill.; Holt Rinehart & Winston, 1978.

Greening, T. "Diversification, Strategic Groups and the Structure-Conduct-Performance Relationship: A Synthesis." *Review of Economics and Statistics*, 62, 1980. pp. 475-477.

Hansen G.S. & Wernerfelt B. "Determinants of Firm Performance: The Relative Importance of Economic and Organizational Factors." *Strategic Management Journal.* Vol. 10, 1989. pp. 399-411.

Harrigan, K.R. "An Application of Clustering for Strategic Group Analysis." *Strategic Management Journal.* 6(1), 1985. pp. 55-74.

Hatten, K.J. and D.E. Schendel. "Heterogeneity Within an Industry." *Journal of Industrial Economics.* XXVI(2), December 1977. pp. 97-113.

Hatten, K.J., D.E. Schendel and A.C. Cooper. "A Strategic Model oft U.S. Brewing Industry: 1952-1971." *Academy of Management Journal.* 21(4), 1978. pp. 592-610.

Hatten, K.J. and M.L. Hatten. "Some Empirical Insights for Strategic Marketers: The Case of Beer." in Thomas, H. and D.M. Gardner (eds), *Strategic Marketing and Management.* John Wiley, Chicester and New York, 1985.

Hatten, K.J. and M.L. Hatten. "Strategic Groups, Asymmetrical Mobility Barriers and Contestability." *Strategic Management Journal.* 8(4). pp. 329-342.

Hawes, J.M. and W.F. Crittenden. "A Taxonomy of Competitive Retailing Strategies." *Strategic Management Journal.* 5(3), 1984. pp. 275-289.

Hergert, M. "The Incidence and Implications of Strategic Groupings in U.S. Manufacturing Industries." unpublished doctoral dissertation, Harvard University, 1983.

Hergert, M. "Causes and Consequences of Strategic Grouping in U.S. Manufacturing Industries." *International Studies of Management & Organization.* Vol. XVIII, No. 1. pp. 26-49.

Howell, R.D. and G.L. Frazier, "Business Definition and Performance." *Journal of Marketing.* 47, Spring 1983. pp. 59-67.

Hunt, M.S. "Competition in the Major Home Appliance Industry 1960-1970." unpublished doctoral dissertation, Harvard University, 1972.

Jemison, D.B. "The Contributions of Administrative Behavior to Strategic Management." *Academy of Management Review.* 6, 1981. pp. 633-42.

Jemison, D.B. "Risk and the Relationship Among Strategy, Organizational Processes, and Performance." *Management Science.* 33,9, 1987. pp. 1087-1101.

Johnston, J. *Econometric Methods.* 2nd edn., McGraw-Hill, New York, New York, 1972.

Jones, R.G., B.T. Lamont and M.W. Pustay. "A Longitudinal Study of Formation and Change in Strategic Groups." Working Paper, Texas A&M University, 1987.

Katz Daniel and Robert Kahn, *The Social Psychology of Organizations.* New York, Wiley, 1978 (2nd ed.).

Klavans Richard, "Scientific Activity, Industry Structure and Firm Strategy." *Academy of Management Best Papers Proceedings 1990.* pp. 22-26.

Lawless, M.W., W.D. Wilsted and D.D. Bergh. "Strategic Groups and Individual Firm Capability: Performance Effects." Working Paper, University of Colorado, 1989.

Lewis P. and H. Thomas. "The Linkage Between Strategy, Strategic Groups and Performance in the U.K. Retail Grocery Industry." *Strategic Management Journal.* September 1990. pp. 385-398.

Lippman, S.A. and R.P. Rumelt. "Uncertainty Imitability: An Analysis of Interfirm Differences in Efficiency Under Competition." *Bell Journal of Economics and Management Science.* August 1982. pp. 418-438.

Mancke, Richard. 'Causes of Interfirm Profitability Differences: A New Interpretation of the Evidence." *Quarterly Journal of Economics.* May 1974. pp. 181-193.

Mascarenhas B. and D.A. Aaker. "Mobility Barriers and Strategic Groups." *Strategic Management Journal.* 10(5) 1989. pp. 475-485.

Mascarenhas B. "Strategic Group Dynamics." *Academy of Management Journal.* Vol.32 (2) 1989. pp. 333-352.

Mason, Edward. "Price and Production Policies of Large-Scale Enterprises." *American Economic Review.* March 1939. pp. 61-7

Mcgee, J. and H. Thomas. "Strategic Groups: A Bridge Between Industry Structure and Strategic Management." in H. Thomas and D.M. Gardner (eds), *Strategic Marketing and Management.* John Wiley, Chichester 1985.

Mcgee, J. and H. Thomas. "Strategic Groups: Theory, Research and Taxonomy." *Strategic Management Journal.* March-April 1986. pp. 141-160.

Mcgee, J. and H. Thomas. "Strategic Groups: Further Comment." *Strategic Management Journal.* 10(1) 1989. pp. 105-107.

Mehra A. "Strategic Groups and Performance in the U.S. Banking Industry." a University of Mass. Working Paper, 1990.

Mehra A. & Floyd S.W. "An Exploration of the Theoretical Rationale for the Existence and Implications of Strategic Groups." a University of Mass. Working Paper, 1992.

Meyer, J.W. & Rowan, B. "Institutionalized Organizations: Formal Structures as Myth and Ceremony." *American Journal of Sociology.* 83:pp. 340-363.

Meyers, S.C. "Finance Theory and Financial Strategy." *Interfaces.* 14,1, 1984. pp. 126-38.

Nayyar, P. "Strategic Groups: A Comment." *Strategic Management Journal.* 10(1) 1989. pp. 101-103.

Neter, J. & Wasserman W. *Applied Linear Statistical Models*. R.D. Irwin, Homewood, IL, 1974.

Newman, H.H. "Strategic Groups and the Structure/Performance Relationship: A Study With Respect to the Chemical Process Industries." unpublished doctoral dissertation, Harvard University, 1973.

Newman, H.H. "Strategic Groups and the Structure/Performance Relationship." *Review of Economics and Statistics*. 60, 1978. pp. 417-427.

Oster, Sharon. "Intraindustry Structure and the Ease of Strategic Changes." *Review of Economics and Statistics*. LXIV(3), August 1982. pp. 376-384.

Penrose, E.G. *The Theory of the Growth of the Firm*. Wiley, New York, 1959.

Porter, M.E. *Interbrand Choice, Strategy, and Bilateral Market Power*. Harvard University Press, Cambridge, 1976.

Porter, M.E. "The Structure Within Industries and Companies' Performance." *Review of Economics and Statistics*. No.61, May 1979. pp. 214-227.

Porter, M.E. *Competitive Strategy*. Free Press, New York, 1980.

Porter, M.E. "The Contributions of Industrial Organization to Strategic Management." *Academy of Management Review*. October 1981. pp. 609-620.

Primeaux, Walter, J. Jr. "A Method for Determining Strategic Groups and Life Cycle Stages of an Industry." in H. Thomas and D.M. Gardner (eds), *Strategic Marketing and Management*. John Wiley, Chichester, 1985.

Quinn, J.B., Doorley, T.L. and Paquette, P.C. "Beyond Products: Services Based Strategy." *Harvard Business Review.* Mar.-Apr. 1990. pp.58-67.

Ramsler, Martin. "Strategic Groups and Foreign Market Entry in Global Banking Competition." unpublished doctoral dissertation, Harvard University, 1982.

Ruefli, T.W. "Mean-Variance Approaches to Risk-Return Relationships in Strategy: Paradox Lost." *Management Science.* Vol. 36, No. 3 March 1990. pp. 368-380.

Ruefli, T.W. "Reply to Bromiley's Comment and Further Results: Paradox Lost Becomes Dilemma Found." *Management Science.* Vol. 37, No.9, September 1991. pp. 1210-1215.

Rumelt, R. "Strategy, Structure and Economic Performance." Division of Research, Graduate School of Business, Harvard University, Boston, MA. 1974.

Schendel, D. and R. Patton. "A Simultaneous Equation Model of Corporate Strategy." *Management Science.* November 1978. pp. 1611-1621.

Scherer, Frederick. *Industrial Market Structure and Economic Performance.* Chicago: Rand McNally, 1972 and 1980.

Shepherd, W.G. "The Elements of Market Structure." *Review of Economics and Statistics,* 54(1), February 1972. pp. 25-37.

Shepherd, W.G. "Contestability vs. Competition." *American Economic Review.* 74, 1984. pp.572-587.

Shepherd, W.G. "Entry Barriers, Contestability and Predatory Pricing." *Revue D'Economie Industrielle.* n 46, 4e trimestre 1988, pp. 1-20.

Snow, C. & Hambrick D. "Measuring Organizational Strategies: Some Theoretical and Methodological Problems." *Academy of Management Review.* 1980. pp. 527-538.

Stigler, G.J. "A Theory of Oligopoly." *Journal of Political Economy.* February 1964. 72 pp. 55-59.

Tassey, Gregory. "Competitive Strategies and Performance in Technology Based Industries." *Journal of Economics and Business.* 1983. pp.21-40.

Thomas, Howard, and Venkatraman N. "Research on Strategic Groups: Progress and Prognosis." *Journal of Management Studies.* Nov. 1988. pp. 537-555.

Wernerfelt, B. "A Resource Based View of the Firm." *Strategic Management Journal.* Vol. 5, 1984. pp. 171-180.

Winn, Daryl. "Industrial Market Structure and Performance." Ann Arbor: Graduate School of Business, The University of Michigan. 1975.

Wright, P. "A Refinement of Porter's Strategies." *Strategic Management Journal.* 8, 1987. pp. 93-101.

Zellner, A. "An Efficient Method of Estimating Seemingly Unrelated Regressions and Tests for Aggregating Bias," *Journal of the American Statistical Society.* 1962. pp. 348-368.

Index